# Getting Started with General and Scanline Materials in 3ds Max 2017®

*ROC*

and

*Elizabeth VT*

RISING POLYGON

Copyright © Rising Polygon

**Book Code:** RPO6C

**Edition:** 2nd Edition

**ISBN:** 978-1536883329

**Web:** www.risingpolgon.co

**Author Email:** rconor@risingpolgon.co

**Color e-Book available at:** www.risingpolgon.co

# Contents

**Acknowledgements**

**About the Author**

**Preface**

This page intentionally left blank

# Acknowledgements

Thanks to:

Everyone at Autodesk [www.autodesk.com].
Everyone at Microsoft [www.microsoft.com].

Thanks to all great digital artists who inspire us with their innovative VFX, gaming, animation, and motion graphics content.

And a very special thanks to wonderful CG artists of London, UK.

Finally, thank you for picking up the book.

# About the Authors

**Rising Polygon**, founded by **Ravi Conor** aka **ROC, Elizabeth VT**, and **Gordon Fisher** is a group of like-minded professionals and freelancers who are specialized in advertising, graphic design, web design and development, digital marketing, multimedia, exhibition, print design, branding, and CG content creation.

**ROC** has over a decade of experience in the computer graphics field and although he is primarily a shading and texturing artist, he is also experienced in the fields of Dynamics, UVMapping, Lighting, and Rendering. Along side 3ds Max, ROC has experience with VRay, Maya, FumeFX, Mudbox, Mari, Photoshop, xNormal, UVLayout, Premiere, and After Effects.

**Elizabeth** is primarily an Android App developer. She is passionate about computer graphics and has an experience of over 6 years with 3ds Max, Maya, Photoshop, and Blender.

**Gordon Fisher** is the back bone of Rising Polygon and handles operations, finance, and accounts.

You can contact authors by sending an e-mail to the following Email ID: **rconor@risingpolygon.co**.

This page intentionally left blank

# Preface

## Why this Book?

The **Getting Started with General and Scanline Materials in 3ds Max 2017, 2ⁿᵈ Edition** textbook offers a hands-on exercises based strategy for all those digital artists who have just started working on the 3ds Max [no experience needed] and interested in learning texturing in 3ds Max.

This brilliant guide takes you step-by-step through the whole process of texturing with General and Scanline materials/maps in 3ds Max. From the very first pages, the users of the book will learn how to effectively use General and Scanline materials/maps in 3ds Max.

## What you need?

To complete the examples and hands-on exercises in this book, you need 2017 version of Autodesk 3ds Max.

## What are the main features of the book?

- The book is written using 3ds Max 2017 in an easy to understand language.
- General and Scanline materials/maps explained.
- 20 Hands-on exercises and practical tests to hone your skills.
- Detailed coverage of tools and features.
- Additional tips, guidance, and advice is provided.
- Important terms are in bold face so that you never miss them.
- Support for the technical aspect of the book.
- 3ds Max files and textures used are available for download from the accompanying website.

## Is this book is available in e-Book format?

Yes. You can download the color e-Book from *www.risingpolygon.co*.

## How This Book Is Structured?

This book is divided into following units:

### Unit MT1-Material Editors

- Compact Material Editor
- Slate Material Editor

### Unit MT2 - General/Scanline Materials and Maps

- General/Scanline materials
- General maps

## Examination Copies

Books received as examination copies are for review purposes only and may not be made available for student use. Resale of the examination copies is prohibited. If you want to receive this book as an examination copy, send the request from your official e-mail id to us using the **Contact** page of from our website.

## Electronic Files

Any electronic file associated with this book are licensed to the original user only. These files can not be transferred to a third party. However, the original user can use these files in personal projects without taking any permission from **Rising Polygon**.

## Trademarks

**3ds Max** is the registered trademarks of **Autodesk Inc**. **Windows** is the registered trademarks of **Microsoft Inc**.

## Disclaimer

All rights reserved. No part of this book may be reproduced, stored in a retrieval system, or transmitted in any form or by any means, without the prior written permission of the publisher, except in the case of brief quotations embedded in critical articles or reviews. No patent liability is assumed with respect to the use of information contained herein. Although every precaution has been taken in the preparation of this book, neither the authors, nor **Rising Polygon**, and its dealers and distributors will be held liable for any damages caused or alleged to be caused directly or indirectly by this book.

All terms mentioned in this book that are known to be trademarks or service marks have been appropriately capitalized. **Rising Polygon** cannot attest to the accuracy of this information. Use of a term in this book should not be regarded as affecting the validity of any trademark or service mark.

## Access to Electronic Files

This book is sold via multiple sales channels. If you don't have access to the resources used in this book, you can place a request for the resources by visiting the following link: *http://bit.ly/resources-rp*.

## Customer Support

At **Rising Polygon**, our technical team is always ready to take care of your technical queries. If you are facing any problem with the technical aspect of the book, navigate to *http://bit.ly/contact-rp* and let us know about your query.

## Reader Feedback

Your feedback is always welcome. Your feedback is critical to our efforts at **Rising Polygon** and it will help us in developing quality titles in the future. To send the feedback, visit *http://bit.ly/contact-rp*.

## Errata

We take every precaution while preparing the content of the book but mistakes do happen. If you find any mistake in this book general or technical, we would be happy that you report it to us so that we can mention it in the errata section of the book's online page. If you find any errata, please report them by visiting the following link: *http://bit.ly/contact-rp*. This will help the other readers from frustration. Once your errata is verified, it will appear in the errata section of the book's online page.

## Contact Author

Stay connected with us through Twitter (**@risingpolygon**) to know the latest updates about our products, information about books, and other related information. You can also send an e-mail to author at the following address: **rconor@risingpolygon.co**.

This page intentionally left blank

# Unit MT1-Material Editors

A material editor is a dialog that allows you to create, and edit materials as well as to assign them to the objects in the scene. A material in 3ds Max defines how light is reflected and transmitted by the objects in a scene.

In the unit, I will describe the following:

- **Compact Material Editor**
- **Slate Material Editor**

3ds Max offers two material editors, **Compact Material Editor** and **Slate Material Editor**. These editors offer a variety of the functions and features that allow you to design realistic looking surfaces in 3ds Max. To open an editor, choose **Compact** ▦ or **Slate** ⸬⤬ option from the **Material Editor** flyout on the **Main** toolbar. You can also open an editor by choosing **Compact Material Editor** or **Slate Material Editor** from the **Rendering** menu | **Material Editor** sub-menu | **Compact Material Editor/Slate Material Editor**. If you are using the enhanced menu system, these options are in the **Material** menu | **Create/Edit Materials** sub-menu.

## Compact Material Editor

This was the only material editor available prior to the 2011 release of 3ds Max. It is comparatively a small dialog [see Figure F1] than the **Slate Material Editor** and allows you to quickly preview the material. If you are assigning materials that have already been designed, this material editor is the preferred choice.

*Note: Additional Features*

*The **Compact Material Editor** has some options such as **Video Color Check** and **Custom Sample Objects** that are not available in the **Slate Material Editor**.*

The **Compact Material Editor's** interface consists of menu bar at the top [see Figure F1], sample slots below the menu bar, and toolbars at the bottom and right of the sample slots. Now onward, I will refer to these toolbars as horizontal and vertical toolbars, respectively. The interface also contains many rollouts. The content on these rollouts depends on the active material slot and the type of material it hosts.

*Note: Switching Editors*

*If you want to switch to **Slate Material Editor**, choose **Slate Material Editor** from the editor's **Modes** menu.*

## Sample Slots

The sample slots allow you to preview material and maps. By default, six sample slots appear in the editor. You can increase the number of slots by choosing **Cycle 3x2, 5x3, 6x4 Sample Slots** from the editor's **Options** menu. This option cycles through the 3x2, 5x3, and 6x4 slots arrangement. To make a sample slot active, click on the sample slot. The active sample slot appears with a white border around it.

*Caution: Maximum number of sample slots*

*The **Compact Material Editor** allows you to edit up to 24 material at a time. However, the scene might contain an unlimited numbers of materials. When you finish a material and apply it to the objects in the scene. You can use the slot occupied by that material to design the next material.*

By default, material appears on a sphere geometry in a sample slot. You can change the sphere to cylinder or cube by choosing the desired option from the **Sample Type** flyout. This flyout is the first entry in the editor's vertical toolbar. To view a magnified version of the sample slot in a floating window, double-click on it. You can resize the window to change the magnification level of the sample slot.

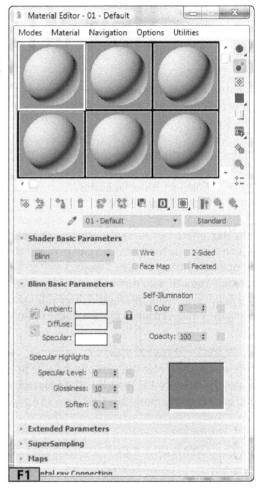

## Hot and Cool Materials

A sample slot is considered to be hot if it is assigned to one or more surfaces in the scene. When you use the editor to adjust properties of a hot material the changes are reflected in the viewport at the same time. The corners of a sample slot indicates whether the material is hot or not. Here are the possibilities:

**No triangle:** The material is not used in the scene.
**Outlined white triangle:** The material is hot and the changes you make to it will change the material displayed in the scene.
**Solid white triangle:** The material is not only hot but it is also applied to the currently selected object in the scene.

Notice the three sample slots in Figure F2 that shows three possibilities: a hot material applied to the currently selected, a hot material is applied to the scene but not on the currently selected object, and a cool material which is active but not assigned to scene, respectively. If you want to make a hot material cool, click **Make Material Copy** from the horizontal toolbar. You can have the same material with the same name in multiple slots but only one slot can be hot. However, you can have more than one hot sample slot as long as each sample slot has a different material.

When you RMB click on a sample slot, a popup menu appears. Table 1 summarizes the options available in this menu.

| **Table 1:** Sample slot RMB click menu | |
| --- | --- |
| Option | Description |
| Drag/Copy | This is on by default. When on, dragging a sample slot copies the material from one sample slot to another. |
| Drag/Rotate | When you select this option, dragging the sample slot rotates the sample geometry in the slot. This is useful in visualizing the map in the slot. |
| Reset Rotation | Resets the sample slot's rotation. |
| Render Map | Opens the **Render Map** dialog that allows you to render the current map. You can create an **AVI** file if the map is animated. |
| Options | Opens the material editor's options. |
| Magnify | Generates a magnified view of the current sample slot. |
| Select By Material | Selects objects based on the material in the sample slot. |
| Highlight Assets in the ATS dialog | This option is typically used for the bitmap textures. It opens the **Asset Tracking** dialog with the assets highlighted. |
| Sample Windows Options | You can use these options to change the number of slots displayed in the material editor. |

## Managing Materials with the Compact Material Editor

By default, the **Standard** material is displayed when you select a sample slot. If you want to use the **Standard** material, you can choose the desired shading model from the drop-down available in the **Shader Basic Parameters** rollout of the editor and then assign colors or maps to the various components of the material. For example, if you want to assign a map to the **Diffuse** component of the material, click on the button located at the right of the **Diffuse** color swatch to open the **Material/Map Browser** which is a modeless dialog. From the browser, select the map from the **Maps | General/Scanline/Environment** rollout and then click **OK**.

*Tip: Material Map Browser*
*You can also double-click on a map to select it and close the browser.*

For example, if you want to apply a checker map, double-click on the **Checker** map from the **Maps | General** rollout of the browser. Once you select the map, 3ds Max shows rollouts in the editor that you can use to edit the properties of the map. To go back to the parent level, click **Go To Parent** from the horizontal toolbar.

You can also copy map from one component to another component. For example, you have applied a map to the **Diffuse** component of the material and you want to copy it to **Opacity** component. Drag the **Diffuse's** button onto the **Opacity's** button, the **Copy (Instance) Map** dialog appears. Select the desired option from the **Method** group and then click **OK** to create an instance, a copy, or just to swap the materials from one slot to another.

*Note: Other materials*
*If you want to use any other material than the **Standard** material, click on **Type** button [currently labelled as **Standard**] to open the **Material/Map Browser**. Double-click on the desired material from the **Materials | General/Scanline** rollout; the **Replace Material** dialog appears with options to discard the old material or keep the old material as a sub-material. Choose the desired option and click **OK**. The label **Standard** on the button will be replaced by the type of the new material. For example, if you have chosen **Blend**, the **Standard** label will be replaced by the **Blend** label.*

By default, 3ds Max gives a name to each material. This appears name below the horizontal toolbar. If you want to change the name, edit the name in the field. The name field only displays 16 characters but the material name can be longer than 16 characters.

If the material you want to change is present in the scene but is not displayed in any of the sample slots, you can get it directly from the scene. To do this, select the object in the scene and click a sample slot to make it active. From the horizontal toolbar, click **Get Material** to open the **Material/Map Browser**. Find the scene material in the **Scene Materials** rollout and then double-click on the name of the material. You can also drag the material name to the sample slot. When you get a material from the scene, it is initially a hot material.

To apply a material to the objects in the scene, drag the sample slot that contains the material to the object[s] in the scene. If there is only one object selected in the scene, the material is immediately applied to that object. If there are more than one objects in the scene, 3ds Max prompts you to choose whether to apply the material to the single object or to the whole selection. You can also apply material to the selection by clicking **Assign Material To Selection** on the horizontal toolbar. Once you apply material to objects in the scene, click **Show Shaded Material in Viewport** on the horizontal toolbar to view the material on the objects in the scene.

*Tip: Hot material*
*When you apply a material to an object, the material becomes a hot material.*

*Tip: Removing material from an object*
*To remove a material from an object, select the object and then execute the following command from the **MAXScript Listener**: $.material=undefined.*

*Note: Selecting objects that have the same material applied*
*From the vertical toolbar, click **Select By Material**. This button will not be available unless the active sample slot contains a material that is applied to the objects in the scene. The **Select Objects** dialog appears. Those objects onto which the material has been applied appear highlighted in the dialog. Click **Select** to select the objects in the scene.*

You can also save a material to the library. A material library helps you in organizing materials. You can use a material from a library in another scene, if required. To save a material to the library, on the horizontal toolbar, click **Put To Library**, the **Put To Library** dialog appears. In this dialog, change the name of the material or leave as is. Click **OK** to save the material. The material is saved in the currently opened library. If no library is open, a new library is created. You can save this library as a file using the **Material/Map Browser** controls.

To get a material from the library, click **Get Material** 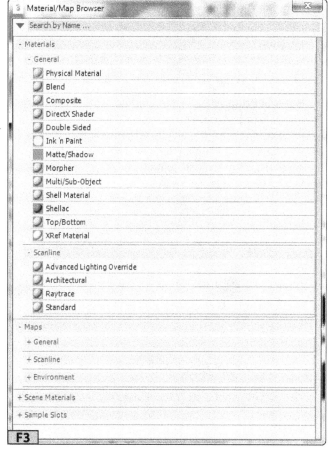 to open the **Material/Map Browser**. Now, open a library group. In the list of the materials in the library, double-click on the name of the material that you intend to use. The material you choose from the library replaces the material in the active sample slot.

## Material/Map Browser

The **Material/Map Browser** [see Figure F3] allows you to choose a material, map, or mental ray shader. When you click the **Type** button or any button on the **Compact Material Editor**, a modal version of the **Material/Map Browser** opens.

*Note: Slate Material Editor*
*In the **Slate Material Editor**, the **Material/Map Browser** appears as a panel and always visible.*

At the top-left corner of the browser, the **Material/Map Browser Options** button ▼ is available. When you click this button, a menu is displayed from where you can set various options for the **Material/Map Browser**. The **Search by Name** field on the right of the button allows you to filter the maps and materials in the browser. For example, if you type **grad** in the field and press **Enter**, the maps and materials will be displayed below the field whose names start with the characters **grad** [see Figure F4].

The main part of the browser is the list of materials and maps arranged in the rollouts [groups]. You can collapse or expand these groups.

F3

F4

*Note: Creating custom groups*

*You can also create custom groups in the browser. To create a group, open the **Material/Map Browser Options** ▼ menu and then choose **New Group**. The **Create New Group** dialog appears. In this dialog, type the name of the group and click **OK**. Now, you can drag the materials or maps from other groups and drop on the new group.*

*Caution: Materials and maps in the Material/Map Browser*

*By default, the **Material/Map Browser** only displays those maps and materials that are compatible with the active renderer.*

*Note: Material/Map Browser's contextual menu*

*When you RMB click on the header of a rollout, a popup menu appears [see Figure F5]. This menu shows the general options related to that particular group.*

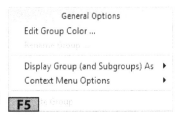

## Material Explorer

The **Material Explorer** [see Figure F6] allows you to browse and manage all materials in a scene. You can open the explorer from the **Rendering** menu. If you are using the enhanced menu system, you can open it from the **Materials** menu | **Tools (Material Set)** sub-menu. You can also open it as an extended viewport. To do this, choose **Material Explorer** from the **Point-Of-View (POV) Viewport** label menu | **Extended Viewports**.

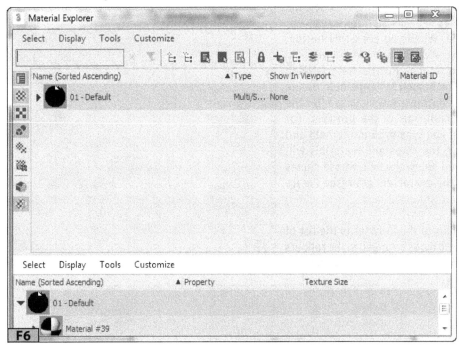

The **Compact Material Editor** lets you set the properties of the materials but there is limitations on number of materials it can display at a time. However, with the **Material Explorer**, you can browse all the materials in the scene. You can also see the objects onto which the materials are applied, you can change the material assignment, and manage materials in other ways.

## Slate Material Editor

The **Slate Material Editor** is little complex than the **Compact Material Editor**. In this editor, the entities are displayed in form of nodes that you can wire together to create material trees. If you are working on a large scene with lots of materials, this editor is the preferred choice. The powerful search function provided by this editor, lets you find materials in a complex scene easily.

I mostly used the **Slate Material Editor** as its interface [see Figure F7] is more intuitive when it comes to designing materials. I have marked various components of the interface with numbers in Figure F7. Table 2 summarizes the **Slate Material Editor's** interface.

| Number | Description |
|--------|-------------|
| Table 2: The **Slate Material Editor's** interface overview | |
| 1 | Menu bar |
| 2 | Toolbar |
| 3 | Material/Map Browser |
| 4 | Status |
| 5 | Active View |
| 6 | View navigation |
| 7 | Parameter Editor |
| 8 | Navigator |

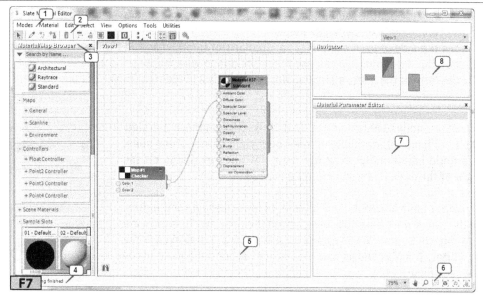

There are three main visual elements of the **Slate Material Editor**: **Material/Map Browser**, **Active View**, and **Parameter Editor**. The **Active View** is the area where you create material trees and make connections between nodes using wires. The **Parameter Editor** is the area where you adjust settings of maps and materials.

You can float the components of the editor such as **Material/Map Browser**, or **Parameter Editor** [except view]. For example, to float the **Material/Map Browser**, double-click on its title. To dock it back to the editor, again double-click on its title.

*Note: Preview window*

*By default, each material preview window opens as a floating window. When you dock a material preview window, it docks to the upper left area of the editor.*

When you add materials or maps in the **Slate Material Editor**, they appear as nodes [see left image in Figure F8] in the active view.

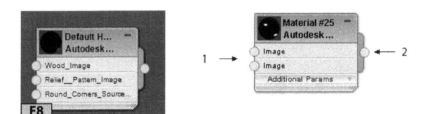

You can then connect these nodes using wires to make material trees. A node has several components, here's is a quick rundown.

- The title bar of the node shows name of the material or map, material or map type, and a small preview icon of the material or map.
- Below the title bar the component of the material or map appear. By default, 3ds Max shows only those components that you can map.
- On the left side of each component a circular slot [marked as 1 in the right image of Figure F8] is available for input. You can use these sockets to wire maps to the node.
- On the right of the node, a circular slot [marked as 2 in the right image of Figure F8] that is used for the socket.

You can collapse a node to hide its slots. To do this, click on the minus sign [marked as 1 in Figure F9] available on the upper right corner of the node. To resize a node horizontally, drag the diagonal lines available on the bottom-right of the node [marked as 2 in Figure F9].

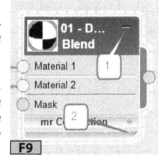

When you resize a node horizontally, it's easier to read the name of the slots. To change the preview icon size, double-click on the preview. To reduce the preview, double-click again. When a node's parameters are displayed in the **Parameter Editor**, 3ds Max shows a dashed border around the node in the active view [see Figure F10].

To create a new material, drag the material from the **Material/Map Browser** to the active view, 3ds Max places a node for the material in the active view. It is a good habit to change the name of the material immediately. It will make your life easier if you are working on a complex scene with tons of materials. To rename a material, RMB click on it and choose **Rename**. In the **Rename** dialog, change the name of the material and click **OK**. To change the properties of the material, double-click the node in the active view and then change the properties from the **Parameter Editor**.

*Tip: Renaming materials*
*The name of a material can contain special characters, numbers, and spaces.*

To get a material from the scene, click **Pick Material From Object** from the toolbar. Now, click on the object in a viewport to get the material. To apply a material to objects in the scene, drag the output socket of the node and then drop the wire on an object in the scene. As you drag the mouse in a viewport, a tooltip appears below the mouse pointer showing the name of the object. You can apply the material even if the object is not selected. If there is only one object selected in the scene, the material is immediately applied to that object. If there are more than one objects in the scene, 3ds Max prompts you to choose whether to apply the material to the single object or to the whole selection. You can also apply material to the selection by clicking **Assign Material To Selection** on the toolbar.

To make a copy of the existing material, drag the material from the **Material/Map Browser | Scene Materials** group (or any library) to the active View. The **Instance (Copy)** dialog appears. Select **Instance** or **Copy** from this dialog and click **OK**. To duplicate a node in the active view, select the node[s] that you want to duplicate and then drag the nodes with the **Shift** held down.

To select the objects onto which you have applied the same material, in the active view, select the node and then click **Select By Material** from the toolbar. 3ds Max opens the **Select Objects** dialog with the objects highlighted. Click **Select** to select the highlighted objects.

### Selecting, Moving, and Laying Out Nodes

To select a node, ensure the **Select Tool** [hotkey **S**] is active, and then click on the node. To select multiple nodes, click on the nodes with the **Ctrl** held down. If you want to remove nodes from the selection, click on the nodes with **Alt** held down. To select all nodes, press **Ctrl+A**. To invert the selection, press **Ctrl+I**. To select none of the nodes, press **Ctrl+D**. To select children, press **Ctrl+C**. To select a node tree, press **Ctrl+T**. These functions are also accessible from the **Select** menu of the editor.

*Note: Selected node*
*When a node is selected in the view, a white border appears around it. Also, the background including the title bar is darker. When node is not selected, the border appears gray and background is lighter.*

*Tip: Deselecting nodes*
*To deselect nodes, click on the blank area of the view using the **Select Tool**.*

To move a node, drag it in the active view. To create clone of a node, drag it with the **Shift** held down. If you drag a node with **Ctrl+Shift** held down, 3ds Max clones the node and all its children. These methods also work on multiple selections.

If you want to move a node and its children, click **Move Children** ⚏ from the toolbar and drag a node. You can toggle this feature temporarily without clicking **Move Children** by moving the node with **Ctrl+Alt** held down. This feature can be accessed from the editor's **Options** menu. You can click the **Hide Unused** ⚏ option from the toolbar to hide the unused ports on the selected material.

The layout buttons on the toolbar allow you to arrange nodes in the active view. The **Layout All - Vertical** ⚏ and **Layout All - Horizontal** ⚏ buttons on the toolbar allow you to arrange nodes in an automatic layout along the vertical or horizontal axis in the active view. These options are also available in the editor's **View** menu. The **Layout Children** button allows you to automatically layout the children of the selected node.

If you turn on the **Show Shaded Material In Viewport** ⚏ from the toolbar for a material, a red diagonal shape appears on the node in the active view [see the left image in Figure F11]. The **Navigator** also shows a red diagonal shape to indicate this [see the middle image in Figure F11]. This shape also appears in the **Scene Materials** rollout of the **Material/Map Browser** [see the right image in Figure F11].

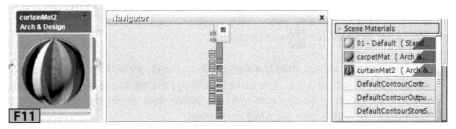

## Previewing Materials

The **Preview** window [see Figure F12] of the editor allows you to visualize how material or map will appear in the scene. The main part of the window is a rendering of the material or map. You can resize this window like you resize any other window in 3ds max that is, by dragging its corners. Making a window larger helps you in visualizing the material, however, larger previews take longer to render. To open this window, RMB click on a node and then choose **Open Preview Window** from the popup menu.

To close a window, click **X** on the upper-right corner of the window. By default, a sphere is displayed as a sample geometry in the scene. If you want to change this geometry, choose **Cylinder** or **Box** from **RMB click** menu | **Preview Object Type** sub-menu. You can open any number of **Preview** windows in the editor. However, the drop-down available at the bottom of the **Preview** window allows you to switch the previews in a single window.

*Caution: Preview window*

*When open a new scene, the **Preview** window remains open, however, it may not correspond to any material. I recommend that you close all **Preview** windows before creating a new scene. The previews are not saved with the scene.*

When the **Auto** switch is on in the **Preview** window, 3ds Max automatically renders the preview again when you make any changes to the properties of a material or map. When this switch is off, the **Update** button becomes active. The render will be displayed only when you click **Update**. The **Show End Result** toggle available on the right of **Update** allows you to control when the **Preview** window displays a map. When off ![icon], the **Preview** window shows the map itself. When on, the **Preview** window shows the end result that is, the final result of the node.

## Wiring Nodes

As you already know, wires are used to connect material or map components. To understand the wiring process, from the **Material/Map Browser | Materials** rollout | **General** rollout, drag **Standard** to the active view to create a **Standard** material node. Similarly, drag **Checker** from the **Material/Map Browser | Maps** rollout | **General** rollout to the active view to create a **Checker** node [see left image in Figure F13]. Click-drag the **Standard** material's **Diffuse Color** socket, a wire appears. Now, drop the wire on the output socket of the **Checker** node to make a connection [see the right image in Figure F13]. You can also connect in reverse. You can connect the output socket of the **Checker** node to the **Diffuse Color** slot of the **Standard** material.

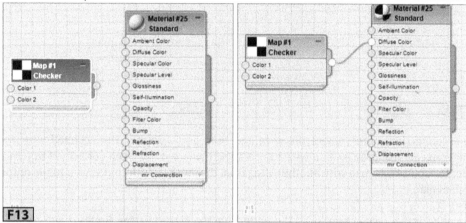

**F13**

Now, drag and the **Standard** material's **Bump** socket to the blank area, a popup menu appears [see the left image in Figure F14], choose **Standard | Noise** from the menu to insert a **Noise** node and make connection between the **Noise** node and **Bump** socket of the **Standard** material [see the right image in Figure F14].

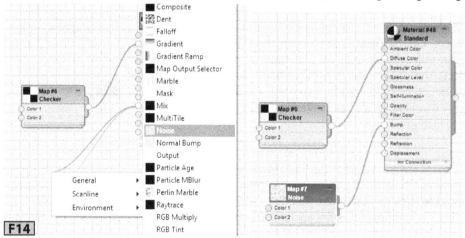

**F14**

You can also connect a map directly to a socket without first dragging to the active view. To do this, drag the **Falloff** map from the **Material/Map Browser | Maps** rollout | **General** rollout to the **Reflection** socket of the **Standard** material. When the socket turns green, release the mouse to make the connection [see Figure

F15]. Another way to connect a node to a socket is that to double-click on a socket to open the **Material/Map Browser**. Now, select the desired map or material from the browser. You can also drag a wire on the title bar of a node. A popup menu appears [see Figure F16] that allows you to select component to wire.

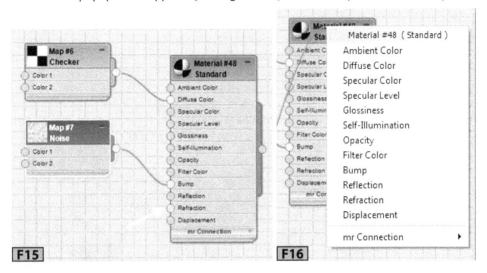

To delete a connection [wire], select the wire and then press **Delete**. The selected wire appears in white color. You can also drag away a wire from a socket where it has been connected to terminate the connection. To replace one map with another, drag from the new map's output socket to the output socket of the original map.

To insert a node into a connection, drag the node from the **Material/Map Browser** and then drop it on the wire. You can also drag from one of the node's input sockets to the wire to insert the node. If a node is lying on the active view and you want to insert it, drop the node on the wire with **Ctrl** held down. To disconnect an inserted node, drag the node and then press **Alt** while dragging.

When you RMB click on a wire, a popup menu appears [see Figure F17]. Choose **Change Material/Map Type** to open the **Material/Map Browser** and then choose a different type for the material or map. This option always affects the child node. The **Make Node Unique** option makes the child unique if the child node is instanced. The **Make Branch Unique** makes the child unique, as well as duplicates children of the child if the child node is instanced.

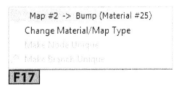

## Views

The active view is the main area of the **Slate Material Editor** where all action takes place. The navigating the active view is similar to the navigating a scene in 3ds Max. To pan the view, drag with the MMB. If you drag with the MMB and **Ctrl+Alt** held down, 3ds max zooms the view. You can also zoom by scrolling the wheel. The navigational tools are also available at the bottom-right corner of the editor's interface.

Table 3 summarized these controls.

| Table 3: The **Slate Material Editor** navigational controls | | |
|---|---|---|
| **Control** | **Hotkey[s]** | **Menu** |
| Zoom percentage drop-down list | - | |
| Pan Tool | Ctrl+P | View \| Pan Tool |
| Zoom Tool | Alt+Z | View \| Zoom Tool |
| Zoom Region Tool | Ctrl+W | View \| Zoom Region Tool |
| Zoom Extents | Ctrl+Alt+Z | View \| Zoom Extents |
| Zoom Extents Selected | Z | Zoom Extents Selected |
| Pan to Selected | Alt+P | View \| Pan to Selected |

If you are working on a complex scene, you might face difficulties locating nodes in the active view. You can use the search function of the editor to locate the nodes in the scene. Make a habit of renaming the nodes as you create them so that you can find the nodes using their names. To search a node, click the **Search For Nodes** button 🔍 available on the bottom-left corner of the active view, 3ds Max expands the search tool. Type the name of the node in the search field and press **Enter** to locate the node and zoom on the node in the active view.

By default, the **Navigator** window appears on the upper-right corner of the **Slate Material Editor**. This window is most useful when you have lots of material trees displayed in the active view. This window shows a map of the active view. The red rectangle in the navigator shows the border of the active view. If you drag the rectangle, 3ds max changes the focus of the view.

### Named Views

If you are working on a complex scene, you can create named views to organize materials in a scene. You can create any number of views in the editor and then make one of them the active view. When you open the editor in a new scene, a single view is displayed with the name **View1**. To manage views, RMB click on one of the tab and then choose the desired options from the popup menu displayed [see Figure F18].

To cycle through the tabs, use the **Ctrl+Tab** hotkeys. You can also select a view from the drop-down available above the **Navigator**. To move a tree from one view to another, RMB click on the node and then choose **Move Tree to View** \| **Name of the View** from the popup menu.

## Summary

The unit covered the following topics:

- **Compact Material Editor**
- **Slate Material Editor**

# Unit MT2 - General/Scanline Materials and Maps

The **General/Scanline Materials** materials are are non-photometric materials. Do not use these materials if you plan to create physically accurate lighting models. However, these materials are suitable for games, films, and animation. In this unit, we are going to look at the standard materials and maps.

In this unit, I'll describe the following:

- General/Scanline materials
- General maps

## General/Scanline Materials

Let's explore the **Scanline** materials.

### Standard Material

A surface having a single color reflects many other colors such as ambient, diffuse, and specular. The **Standard** materials use a four-color model to simulate the reflected colors from a surface. However, there may be variations depending on the shader you use. The **Ambient** color appears where surface is lit (the surface in the shadow) by the ambient light only. The **Diffuse** color appears on the surface when the lights falls directly on it. The term **Diffuse** is used because light is reflected in various directions. The **Specular** color appears in the highlights. Highlights are reflection of light sources on the surface.

Generally, shiny surfaces have specular highlights where the viewing angle is equal to the angle of incident. Metallic surfaces show another type of highlights called glancing highlights. The glancing highlights have a high angle of incidence. Some surfaces in the real-world are highly reflective. To model such surfaces, you can use a reflection map or use raytracing. The **Filter Color** is the color transmitted through an object. The **Filter Color** will only be visible, if **Opacity** is less than **100** percent.

The three color components blend at the edge of their respective regions. The **blend** of the **Diffuse** and **Ambient** components is controlled by the shader. However, you can control the blending by using the **Standard** material's highlight controls.

To create a **Standard** material, press **M** to open the **Slate Material Editor**. On the **Material Editor | Material /Map Browser | Materials | Scanline** rollout, double-click **Standard** to add a standard material node to the active view. Figure F1 shows the **Standard** material's interface. If you double-click on the material node, its attributes appear in various rollouts on the **Parameter Editor**. The controls on these rollouts change according to the shader type chosen from the **Shader Basic Parameters** rollout [see Figure F2].

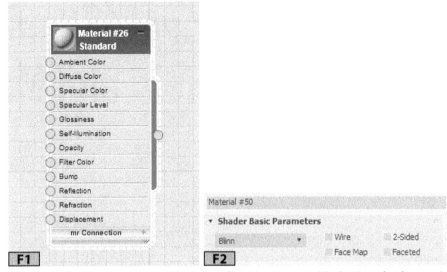

F1

F2

The controls in this rollout let you choose the type of shader to use with the **Standard** material. **Wire** lets you render the material in the wireframe mode [see Figure F3]. You can change the size of the wire using the **Size** control on the material's **Extended Parameters** rollout. Figure F4 shows the render with **Size** set to **2**. **2-Sided** allows you to make a 2-sided material. When you select this option, 3ds Max applies material to the both sides of the selected faces.

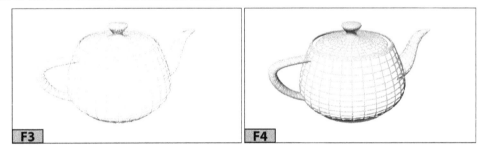

F3

F4

*Note: One-sided faces*

*In 3ds Max, faces are one-sided. The front side is the side with the surface normals. The back side of the faces is invisible to the renderer. If you see this other side from the back, the faces will appear to be missing.*

The **Face Map** control allows you to apply the material to the faces of the geometry. If material is a mapped material, it requires no mapping coordinates and automatically applied to each face. Figures F5 and F6 show the render with the **Face Map** switch is in off and on states, respectively. The **Faceted** control renders each face of the surface as if it were flat [see Figure F7].

*Tip: Rendering both sides of a face*

*There are two ways to render both sides of a face. Either you can turn on **Force 2-Sided** in the **Render Setup** dialog | **Common** panel | **Options** section or apply a two sided material to the faces.*

The **Shader** drop-down located at the extreme left of the rollout lets you choose a shader for the material.

Here's is the quick rundown to the various material shaders:

## Phong Shader

You can use this shader to produce realistic highlights for shiny, and regular surfaces. This shader produces strong circular highlights. This shader can accurately render bump, opacity, shininess, specular, and reflection maps. When you select the **Phong** shader, the **Phong Shader Parameters** rollout appears in the material's **Parameter Editor** [see Figure F8].

## Phong Shader Parameters Rollout

The controls in this rollout, let you set the color of the material, shininess, and transparency of the material. The **Ambient**, **Diffuse**, and **Specular** controls let you set the colors for ambient, diffuse, and specular color components, respectively. To change a color component, click on the color swatch and then use the **Color Selector** to change the values of the color component. You can also copy one color component to another by dragging the source color swatch to the target color swatch. In the **Copy or Swap Colors** dialog that appears, click **Swap**, or **Copy** button. Click **Cancel** to cancel the operation. You can lock or unlock two color components using the **Lock** button [see Figure F9].

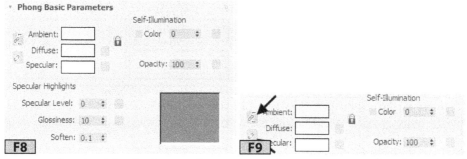

The buttons located on the right of color swatches can be used to apply texture maps to the respective color components. On clicking these buttons, the **Material/Map Browser** appears that allows you to select a map for the color component. If you want to apply different maps to the **Ambient** and **Diffuse** components, click on the **Lock** button located to the right of these components [see Figure F10].

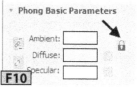

**Self-Illumination Group:** You can use the controls in this group to make the material self-illuminated. The illusion of self-illumination is created by replacing shadows with the diffuse color. There are two ways to enable self-illumination in 3ds Max. Either you can turn on the switch located in this group and use a self-illumination color or use the spinner.

*Note: Self-illuminated materials*
*Self-illuminated materials do not show shadows cast onto them. Also, they are unaffected by the lights in the scene.*

**Opacity Group:** You can use the controls in this group, to make a material opaque, transparent, or translucent. To change the opacity of the material, change opacity to a value less than 100%. If you want to use a map for controlling opacity, click **Opacity** map button.

**Specular Highlight Group: Phong**, **Blinn**, and **Oren-Nayar-Blinn** shaders produce circular highlights and share same highlight controls. **Blinn** and **Oren-Nayar-Blinn** shaders produce soft and round highlights than the **Phong** shader. You can use the **Specular Level** control to increase or decrease the strength of a highlight. As you change the value for this control, the **Highlight** curve and the highlight in the preview changes. The shape of this curve affects the blending between the specular and diffuse color components of the material. If the curve is steeper, there will be less blending and the edge of the specular highlight will be sharper. To increase or decrease the size of the highlight, change the value for **Glossiness**. **Soften** softens the specular highlights especially those formed by the glancing light.

### Extended Parameters Rollout

The **Extender Parameters** rollout [see Figure F11] is same for all shaders except **Strauss** and **Translucent** shaders. The controls in this rollout allow you to control the transparency and reflection settings. Also, it has controls for adjusting the wireframe rendering.

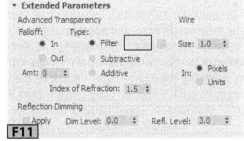

**Advanced Transparency Group:** These controls do not appear for the **Translucent** shader. **Falloff** allows you to set the falloff and its extent. **In** increases transparency toward the inside of the object (like glass bottle) whereas **Out** increases transparency toward the outside of the object (like clouds). **Amt** lets you adjust the amount of transparency at the outside or inside extreme.

The **Type** controls let you specify how transparency is applied. The **Filter** color swatch computes a filter color that it multiplies with the color behind the transparent surface. The **Subtractive** option subtracts from the color behind the transparent surface. The **Additive** option adds to the color behind the transparent surface.

**Index of Refraction** allows you to set the index of refraction used by refraction map and raytracing.

**Reflection Dimming group:** This group does not appear for the **Strauss** shader. These controls dim the reflection in shadow. Tun on the **Apply** switch to enable reflection dimming. **Dim Level** controls the amount of dimming that takes place in shadow. **Refl. Level** affects the intensity of the reflection that is not in shadow.

### SuperSampling Rollout

The **SuperSampling** rollout [see Figure F12] is used by the **Architectural, Raytrace, Standard,** and **Ink 'n Paint** materials to improve the quality of the rendered image. It performs an additional antialiasing pass on the material thus resulting in more render time. By default, a single **SuperSampling** method is applied to all materials in the scene.

*Note: Super Sampling*
*The **Super Sampling** method is ignored by **mental ray** as it has its own sampling algorithm.*

*Caution: Super Sampling and Scanline Renderer*
*If you turn off **Antialiasing** on the default **Scanline Renderer** rollout, **SuperSampling** settings are ignored.*

**Maps Rollout:** The **Maps** rollout [see Figure F13] is available for all materials. The controls in this rollout allow you to assign maps to various components of the material. To assign map to a component, click a map button. Now, choose the desired map option from the **Material/Map Browser** that opens.

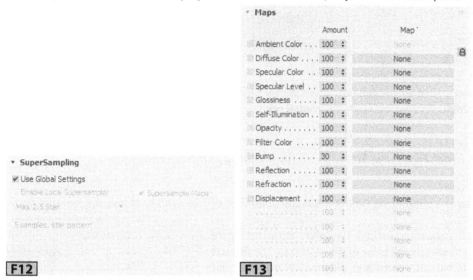

Blinn Shader
This is the default shader. It produces rounder, softer highlights than the **Phong** shader. The **Blinn** and **Phong** shaders have the same basic parameters.

Metal Shader
You can use the **Metal** shader to create realistic-looking metallic surfaces and a variety of organic-looking materials. The metal material calculates their specular color automatically. The output specular color depends on the diffuse color of the material and the color of the light.

This shader produces distinctive highlights. Like the **Phong** shader, **Specular Level** still controls intensity. However, **Glossiness** affects both the intensity and size of the specular highlights. Figure F14 shows the controls in **Metal Basic Parameters** rollout.

Oren-Nayar-Blinn Shader
This shader is a variant of the **Blinn** shader and can be used to model matte surfaces such as fabric. It has two additional controls to model a surface with the matte look: **Diffuse Level** and **Roughness**.

**[Oren-Nayar-Blinn Basic Parameters rollout | Advanced Diffuse Group]: Diffuse Level** controls [see Figure F15] the brightness of the diffuse component of the material. It allows you to make the material lighter or darker. **Roughness** allows you to control the rate at which the diffuse component blends into the ambient component.

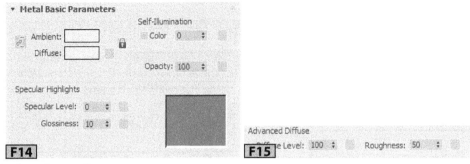

**F14**  **F15**

*Note: The Roughness Parameter*

The **Roughness** *parameter is available only with the* **Oren-Nayar-Blinn** *and* **Multi-Level** *shaders, and with the* **Arch & Design** *and* **Physical** *materials (***mental ray***).*

*Note: Diffuse Level control*

The **Blinn**, **Metal**, **Phong**, *and* **Strauss** *shaders do not have the* **Diffuse Level** *control.*

### Strauss Shader

This shader is a simpler version of the **Metal** shader. It can be used to model the metallic surfaces.

**Strauss Basic Parameters Rollout:** The **Color** control [see Figure F16] lets you specify the color of the material. The **Strauss** shader automatically calculates the ambient and specular color components. **Glossiness** controls the size and intensity of the specular highlights. On increasing the value for this control, the highlight gets smaller and the material appears shiner. The **Metalness** control adjust the

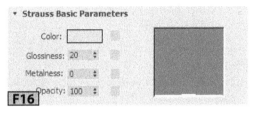

metalness of the surface. The effect of this control is more prominent when you increase the **Glossiness** value. **Opacity** sets the transparency of the material.

### Anisotropic Shader

You can use this shader to create surfaces with elliptical, anisotropic highlights. This shader is suitable for modeling hair, glass, or brushed metal. The **Diffuse Level** controls are similar to that of the **Oren-Nayar-Blinn** shading controls, and basic parameters controls are similar to that of the **Blinn** or **Phong** shading, except the **Specular Highlights** parameters.

**Anisotropic Basic Parameters Rollout | Specular Highlight Group:** The **Specular Level** [Figure F17] control sets the intensity of the specular highlights. On increasing the value for this control, the highlight goes brighter. **Glossiness** controls the size of the specular highlights. The **Anisotropy** controls the anisotropy or shape of the highlight. **Orientation** controls the orientation of the highlight. This value is measured in degrees.

### Multi-Layer Shader

This shader is similar to the **Anisotropic** shader. However, it allows you to layer two sets of specular highlights. The highlights are layered that allows you to create complex highlights. Figure F18 shows the two specular layers in the **Multi-Layer Basic Parameters** rollout.

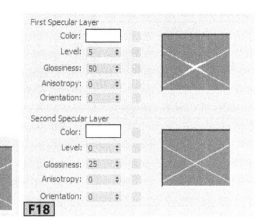

**Specular Highlight**
Specular Level: 5
Glossiness: 25
Anisotropy: 50
Orientation: 0

**F17**

**F18**

### Translucent Shader

This shader is similar to the **Blinn** shader but allows you set the translucency of the material. A translucent object not only allows light to pass through but it also scatters light within.

**Translucent Basic Parameters Rollout | Translucency Group:** The **Translucent Clr** control [see Figure F19] sets the translucency color that is the color of the light scattered within the material. This color is different from the **Filter** color which

**F19**

is the color transmitted through transparent or semi-transparent material such as glass. The **Opacity** control sets the opacity or transparency of the material.

*Note: The mental ray renderer*

*The **mental ray** renderer is used in hands-on-exercises of this book.*

### Raytrace Material

This material is an advanced surface-shading material. It supports the same diffuse surface shading that a **Standard** material supports.

However, it also supports fog, color density, translucency, fluorescence, and other special effects. This material is capable of creating fully raytraced reflections and refractions. Figure F20 shows the **Raytrace** material's interface.

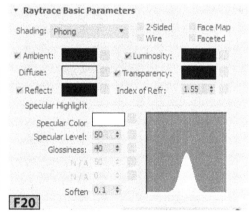

**F20**

### Architectural Material

The properties of this material [see Figure F21] create realistic looking images when used with Photometric lights and Radiosity. Therefore, you should use this material when you are looking for high level of accuracy. If you don't need the high detail this material produces, use the Standard material or any other material.

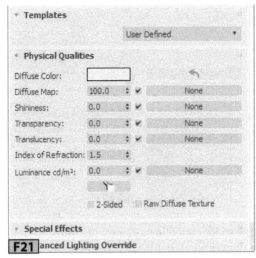

F21 anced Lighting Override

When you create a new **Architectural** material, you can choose from a wide variety of templates that are built into this material. You can use these templates as starting point for the shading model you wish to create. You can choose template from the drop-down available in the **Templates** rollout.

## Advanced Lighting Override Material

You can use this material to directly control the radiosity properties of a material. You can use this material directly. It is a always a supplement to the base material [see Figure F22]. This material has no effect on the ordinary renderings. It is used with Radiosity and Light Tracing solutions.

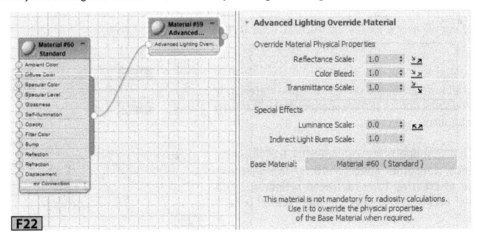

F22

This material has two primary usages:

*   Adjusting properties of a material used in a Radiosity and Light Tracing solutions.
*   Contributing energy to the Radiosity solution with self-illuminating objects.

*Caution: The mental ray renderer*
*The **mental ray** renderer does not support this material.*

# General Materials

Let's explore the **General** materials.

## Blend Material

The **Blend** material allows you to mix two materials on a single side of the surface. You can use the **Mix Amount** parameter [see Figure F23] to control the way two materials are blended together. You can also animate this control. The **Material 1** and **Material 2** controls let you assign the two materials to be blended. You can also use the corresponding switches to turn material on or off. The **Interactive** option specifies which of the materials or mask map will be displayed in the viewport by the interactive renderer.

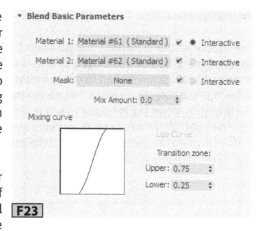

The **Mask** control lets you assign a map as mask. The lighter and darker areas on the mask map control the degree of blending. The lighter areas displays more of the **Material 1** whereas the darker areas show more of **Material 2**. The **Mix Amount** controls the proportion of blend in degrees. A value of **0** means only **Material 1** will be visible on the surface whereas a value of **100** means **Material 2** will be visible on the surface.

**F23**

When you assign a mask map for blending, you can use the mixing curve to affect the blending. You can use the controls in the **Transition Zone** group to adjust the level of the **Upper** and **Lower** limits.

*Note: Interactive renderer and Blend material*
*Only one map can be displayed in the viewports when using the interactive renderer.*

*Note: Blend Material and Noise Map*
*The **Mix Amount** control is not available when you use mask to blend the material. Using a **Noise** map as mixing map can produce naturally looking surfaces.*

## Double Sided Material

The **Double Sided** material lets you assign two different materials to the front and back surface of an object. The **Facing Material** and **Back Material** controls [see Figure F24] allow you to specify the material for the front and back faces, respectively. The **Translucency** control allows you to blend the two materials. There will be no blending of the materials if **Translucency** is set to **0**. At a value of **100**, the outer material will be visible on the inner faces and inner material will be visible on the outer faces.

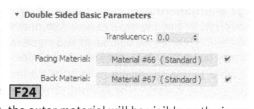

**F24**

## Composite Material

This material can be used to composite up to ten materials. The materials are composited from top to bottom. The maps can be combined using additive opacity, subtractive opacity, or using an amount value. The **Base Material** control [see Figure F25] allows you to set the base material. The default base material is the **Standard** material.

The **Mat.1** to **Mat.9** controls are used to specify the material that you want to composite. Each material control has an array of buttons called **ASM** buttons. These buttons control how the material is composited. The **A** button allows you to use the additive opacity.

The colors in the materials are summed based on the opacity. The **S** button allows you to use the subtractive opacity. The **M** button is used to mix the materials using a value. You can enter the value in the spinner located next to the **M** button. When the **M** button is active, amount ranges from **0** to **100**. When amount is **0**, no compositing happens and the material below is not visible. If the amount is **100**, the material below is visible.

*Tip: Composite Material v Composite Map*
*If you want to achieve a result by combining maps instead of combining materials, use the **Composite** map that provides greater control.*

*Note: Overloaded compositing*
*For additive and subtractive compositing, the amount can range from **0** to **200**. When the amount is greater than **100**, the compositing is overloaded. As a result, the transparent area of the material becomes more opaque.*

## Morpher Material

The **Morpher** material is used with the **Morpher** modifier. For example, when a character raises his eyebrows, you can use this material to display wrinkles on his forehead. You can blend the materials the same way you morph the geometry using the channel spinners of the **Morpher** modifier.

## Multi/Sub-Object Material

The **Multi/Sub-Object** material allows you to assign materials at the sub-object level. The number field [see Figure F26] shows the number of sub-materials contained in the **Multi/Sub-Object** material. You can use the **Set Number** button to set the number of sub-materials that make up the material. The **Add** button allows you to a new sub-material to the list. Use the **Delete** button to remove currently chosen sub-material from the list. The **ID**, **Name**, and **Sub-Material** controls allow you to sort the list based on the material id, name, and sub-material, respectively.

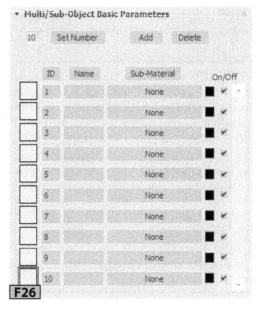

To assign materials to the sub-objects, select the object and assign the **Multi/sub-Object** material to it. Apply a **Mesh Select** modifier to the object. Activate the **Face** sub-object level. Now, select the faces to which you will assign the material. Apply a **Material Modifier** and then set the material ID value to the number of the sub-material you need to assign.

## Shellac Material

**Shellac** material allows you to mix two materials by superimposing one over the other. The superimposed material is known as the **Shellac** material. The **Base Material** control [Figure F27] lets you choose or edit the base sub-material. The **Shellac Material** control lets you choose or edit the **Shellac** material. The **Shellac Color Blend** control adjusts the amount of color mixing. The default value for this control is **0**. Hence, the **Shellac** material has

no effect on the surface. There is no upper limit for this control. Higher values overload the colors of the **Shellac** material. You can also animate this parameter.

## Top/Bottom Material

This material lets you assign two different materials to the top and bottom portions of an object. You can also blend the two materials. The top faces of an object are those faces whose normals point up. The bottom faces have the normals down. You can control the boundary between the top and bottom using the controls available in the **Coordinates** group [see Figure F28].

The **World** option lets you specify the direction according to the world coordinates of the scene. If you rotate the object, the boundary between the top and bottom faces remains in place. The **Local** option allows you to control the direction using the local coordinate system.

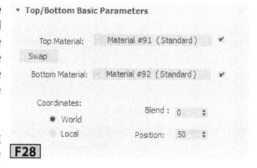

You can specify the top and bottom materials using the **Top** and **Bottom** controls, respectively. The **Swap** button allows you to swap the material. You can blend the edge between the top and bottom materials using the **Blend** control. The value for this control ranges from **0** to **1**. If you set **Blend** to **0**, there will be a sharp line between the top and bottom materials. At **100**, the two materials tint each other.

The **Position** control allows you to specify the location where the division between the two materials will occur. The value for this control ranges from **0** to **1**. If you set **Position** to **0**, only top material will be displayed. At **100**, only bottom material will be displayed.

## Matte/Shadow Material

The **Matte Shadow** material is used to make whole objects or any set of faces into matte objects. The matte objects reveal the background color or the environment map. A matte object is invisible but it blocks any geometry behind it however it does not block the background. The matte objects can also receive shadows. The shadows cast on the matte object are applied to the alpha channel. To properly generate shadows on a matte object, turn off **Opaque Alpha** and then turn on **Affect Alpha**.

### Ink 'n Paint Material

The **Ink 'n Paint** material is used to create cartoons effects. This material produces shading with inked borders.

### DirectX Shader Material

It is a special material that allows you to shade objects in the viewport using DirectX (Direct3D) shaders. When you use this material, materials in the viewport more accurately represent how they will look on some other software or hardware device.

*Tip: Quicksilver hardware renderer*
*You can use the **Quicksilver hardware renderer** to render **DirectX Shader** materials.*

### XRef Material

This material lets you use a material applied to an object in another 3ds Max scene file. This material is typically used with the XRef objects. You can also use the **Override Material** rollout to assign a local material to the XRef'd object.

### Physical Material

**Physical** material allows you to model shading effects of the real-world materials with ease. This material is the layered material that gives you ability to efficiently use the physically-based workflows. This material is compatible with **ART** and **mental ray** renderers.

## General/Scanline Maps

Maps allow you to improve the appearance of the materials. They also help you to enhance the realism of the materials. You can use maps in a variety of ways, you can use them to create environments, to create image planes for modeling, to create projections from light, and so forth. You can use the **Material/Map Browser** to load a map or create a map of a particular type. A map can be used to design different elements of a material such as reflection, refraction, bump, and so forth.

### Maps and Mapping Coordinates

When you apply a map to any object, the object must have mapping coordinates applied. These coordinates are specified in terms of UVW axes local to the object. Most of the objects in 3ds Max have the **Generate Mapping Coordinates** option. When on, 3ds Max generates default mapping coordinates.

### UVW Mapping Coordinate Channels

Each object in 3ds Max can have **99** UVW mapping coordinates. The default mapping is always assigned the number **1**. The **UVW Map** modifier can send coordinates to any of these **99** channels.

3ds Max gives you ability to generate the mapping coordinates in different ways:

- The **Generate Mapping Coords** option is available for most of the primitives. This option provides a projection appropriate to the shape of the object type.
- Apply the **Unwrap UVW** modifier. This modifier comes with some useful tools that you can use to edit mapping coordinates.
- Apply the **UVW Map** modifier. This modifier allows you to set a projection type from several projection types it provides.

Here's the quick rundown to the projection types:

- **Box projection:** It places a duplicate of the map image on each of the six sides of a box.

- **Cylindrical projection:** This wraps the image around the sides of the object. The duplicate images are also projected onto the end caps.

- **Spherical projection:** This projection type wraps the map image around a sphere and gather the image at the top and bottom.

- **Shrink-wrap projection:** This type is like the spherical projection but creates one singularity instead of two.

- Use special mapping coordinates. For example, the **Loft** object provides built-in mapping coordinates.
- Use a **Surface Mapper** modifier. This modifier uses a map assigned to a NURBS surface and projects it onto the object(s).

Here's quick rundown to the cases when you can apply a map and you don't need mapping coordinates:

- Reflection, Refraction, and Environment maps.
- 3D Procedural maps: **Noise** and **Marble**.
- Face-mapped materials.

*Tip: UVW Remove utility*
*The **UVW Remove** utility removes mapping coordinates or materials from the currently selected objects. The path to the utility is as follows: **Utilities** panel | **Utilities** rollout | **More** button | **Utilities** dialog | **UVW Remove**. You can also remove material from objects using the **UVW Remove** utility.*

## Real-World Mapping
The real-world mapping is an alternative mapping method that you can use in 3ds Max. This type of mapping considers the correct scaling of the texture mapped materials applied to the geometry in the scene.

*Note: Autodesk Materials*
*Autodesk materials require you to use the real-world mapping.*

In order to apply the real-world mapping correctly, two requirements must be met. First, the correct style of UV texture coordinates must be assigned to the geometry. In other words, the size of the UV space should correspond to the size of the geometry. To address this issue, the **Real-World Map Size** switch is added to the many rollouts in 3ds Max [see Figure F29].

The second requirement is available in the **Coordinates** rollout of the **Material Edito**, the **Use Real-World Scale** switch. When this switch is on, **U/V** changes to **Width/Height** and **Tiling** changes to **Size** [see Figure F30].

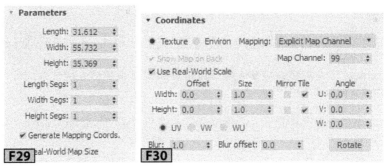

*Note: Real-world Mapping*
*The real-world mapping is off in 3ds Max, by default.*

*Tip: Real-World Map Size check box*
*You can turn on **Real-World Map Size** by default from the **Preferences** dialog by using the **Use Real-World Texture Coordinates** switch. This option is available in the **Texture Coordinates** section of the **General** panel.*

## Output Rollout

The options in this rollout [see Figure F31] are responsible for setting the internal parameters of a map. These options can be used to determine the rendered appearance of the map. Most of the controls on this rollout are for the color output.

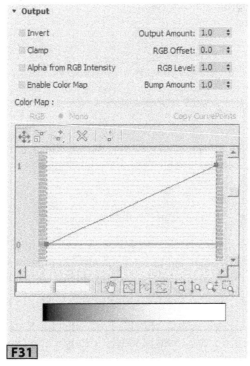

*Note: Output Rollout*
*These controls do not affect the bump maps except the **Invert** toggle, which reverses the direction of the bumps and bump amount.*

### 2D Maps

The 2D maps are two-dimensional images that are mapped to the surface of the geometric objects. You can also use them to create environment maps. The **Bitmap** is the simplest type 2D maps. 3ds Max also allows you to create 2D maps procedurally.

### Coordinates Rollout

The **Coordinates** rollout shown in Figure F30 allows you to adjust coordinate parameters to move a map relative to the surface of the object. This rollout also allows you to set tiling and mirroring of the texture pattern. The repetition of the texture pattern on the surface of an object is known as tiling. The mirroring is a form of tiling in which 3ds Max repeats the map and then flips the repeated map.

In this rollout, there are two options that you can use to control the mapping type. These options are **Texture** and **Environ**. The **Texture** type applies texture as a map to the surface. The **Environ** type uses map as an environment map. For both of these options, you can select the types of coordinates from the **Mapping** drop-down.

Here's the list of options available in the **Mapping** drop-down:

- **Explicit Map Channel:** It uses any map channel from **1** to **99**. When you select this option, **Map Channel** becomes active.
- **Vertex Color Channel:** This option uses assigned vertex colors as a channel.
- **Planar from Object XYZ:** This option uses planar mapping based on the object's local coordinates.
- **Planar from World XYZ:** This option uses planar mapping based on the scene's world coordinates.
- **Spherical Environment/Cylindrical Environment/Shrink-wrap Environment:** These options project the map into the scene as if it were mapped to an invisible object in the background.
- **Screen:** This option projects a map as a flat backdrop in the scene.

### Noise Rollout

You can add a random noise to the appearance of the material using the parameters available in this rollout [see Figure F32]. These parameters modify the mapping of pixels by applying a fractal noise function.

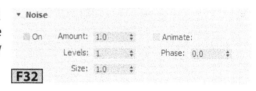

### Bitmap

This map is the simplest type of map available in 3ds Max. This map is useful for creating many type of materials from wood to skin. If you want to create an animated material, you can use an animation or video file with this map. When you select this map, the **Select Bitmap Image File** dialog opens. Navigate to the location where the bitmap file is stored and then click **Open** to select the file.

*Tip: Bitmap and Windows Explorer*
*You can also create a bitmap node by dragging a supported bitmap file from* **Windows Explorer** *to the* **Slate Material Editor***.*

*Tip: Viewport Canvas*
*The* **Viewport Canvas** *feature allows you create a bitmap on the fly by painting directly onto the surface of the object. To open the canvas, choose* **Viewport Canvas** *from the* **Tools** *menu.*

## Checker Map

This map is a procedural texture that applies a two-color checkerboard pattern [see Figure F33]. The default colors used to produce the pattern are black and white. You can also change these colors with map and it's true for all color components of the other maps.

## Camera Map Per Pixel Map

This map allows you to project a map from the direction of a particular camera. It is useful when you are working on a matte painting. Figure F34 shows the **Marble** map projected on the teapot using the camera [see Figure F35]. Figure F36 shows the node network.

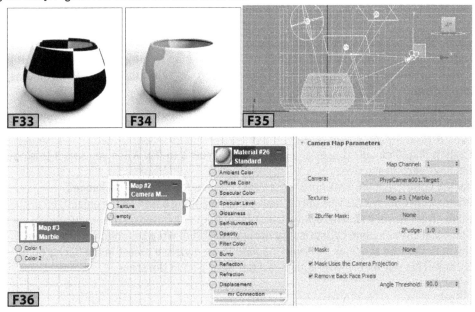

*Note: Two maps with the sane name*
*If a map with the same name exists in two places, only one map is loaded to save the loading time. If you have two maps with different contents but with the same name, only the first map encountered by 3ds Max appears in the scene.*

*Tip: Swapping Colors*
*You can swap colors by dragging one color swatch over another and then choosing **Swap** from the popup menu.*

*Warning: Camera Map Per Pixel Map*
*This map cannot be used with the animated objects or animated textures.*

## Gradient Map

This map type allows you to create a gradient that shades from one color to another. Figure F37 shows the shift from one color to another. The red, green, and blue colors are used for the gradient. Figure F38 shows the result when the fractal noise is applied to the gradient. Figure F39 shows the node network.

## Gradient Ramp Map

This map is similar to the **Gradient** map. Like the **Gradient** map, it shades from one color to another, however, you can use any number of colors [see Figure F40]. Also, you have additional controls to create a complex customized ramp. Figure F41 shows the node network used to produce the result shown in Figure F40.

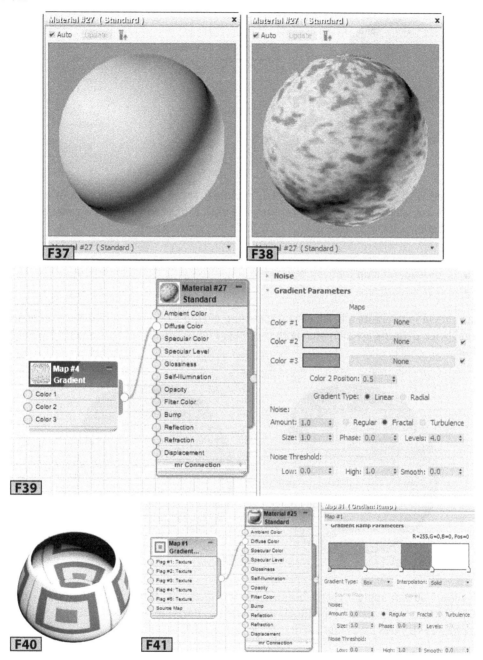

F37

F38

F39

F40

F41

Normal Bump Map

This map allows you to connect a texture-baked normal map to a material. Figure F42 shows the bump on the surface created using the **Normal Bump** map. Figure F43 shows the node network.

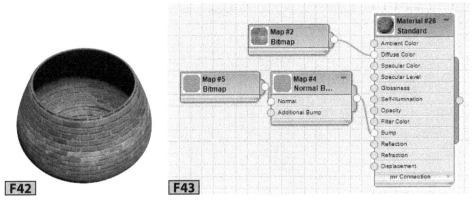

F42    F43

### Substance Map

This map is used with the **Substance** parametric textures. These textures are resolution-independent 2D textures and use less memory. Therefore, they are useful for exporting to the game engines via the **Algorithmic Substance Air** middleware.

### Swirl Map

This map is 2D procedural map that can be used to simulate swirls [see Figure F44].

### Tiles Map

You can use this map to create a brick or stacked tiling of colors or maps. A number of commonly used architectural brick patterns are available with this map. Figure F45 shows render with the **English Bond** type applied.

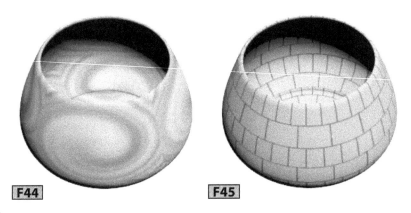

F44    F45

### Vector Map

Using this map, you can apply a vector-based graphics, including animation as textures. You can also use **AutoCAD Pattern** (PAT) files, **Adobe Illustrator** (AI) files, **Portable Document** (PDF) files, and **Scalable Vector Graphics** (SVG) files [see Figure 46].

### Vector Displacement Map

This map allows you to displace the meshes in three directions whereas the traditional method permits displacement only along the surface normals.

3D maps are patterns generated by 3ds Max in 3D space. Let's have a look at various 3D maps.

## Cellular Map

You can use this map to generate a variety of visual effects such as mosaic tiling, pebbled surfaces, and even ocean surfaces [see Figure F47].

## Dent Map

This map generated a procedural map using a fractal noise algorithm. The effect that this produces depends on the map type chosen.

## Falloff Map

The **Falloff** map generates a value from white to black based on the angular falloff of the face normals. Figure F48 shows the **Falloff** map applied to the geometry with the **Falloff** type set to **Fresnel**.

F46

F47

F48

## Marble Map

You can use this map to create a marble texture with the colored veins against [see Figure F49] a color background.

## Noise Map

This map allows to create a noise map that creates the random perturbation of a surface based on the interaction of two colors or materials. Figure F50 shows the **Noise** map with the **Noise Type** set to **Fractal**.

## Particle Age Map

This map is used with the particle systems. This map changes the color of the particles based on their age.

## Particle MBlur Map

This map can be used to alter the opacity of the leading and trailing ends of particles based on their rate of motion.

## Perlin Marble Map

This map is like the **Marble** map. However, it generates a marble pattern using the **Perlin Turbulence** algorithm.

## Smoke Map

You can use this map [see Figure F51] to create animated opacity maps to simulate the effects of smoke in a beam of light, or other cloudy, flowing effects.

## Speckle Map
This map [see Figure F52] can be used to create granite-like and other patterned surfaces.

## Splat Map
This map can be used to create patterns similar to the spattered paint [see Figure F53].

## Stucco Map
You can use this map [see Figure F54] as a bump to create the effect like a stuccoed surface.

## Waves Map
You can use this map as both bump or diffuse map [see Figure F55]. This map is used to create watery or wavy effects.

## Wood Map
This map creates a wavy grain like wood pattern [see Figure F56]. You can control the direction, thickness, and complexity of the grain.

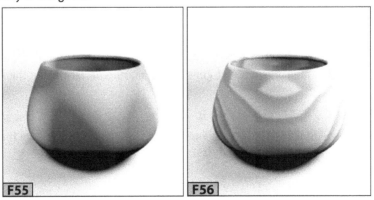

## Compositor Maps

These maps are specifically designed for compositing colors and maps. Let's have a look at these maps.

### Composite Map

You can use this map to layer other maps atop each other using the alpha channel and other methods.

### Mask Map

This map can be used to view one material through another on the surface.

### Mix Map

With this map, you can combine two colors or materials on a single side of the surface. You can also animate the **Mix Amount** parameter to control how two maps are blended together over time.

### RGB Multiply Map

This map combines two maps by multiplying their RGB values. This map is generally used as a **Bump** map.

## Color Modifiers Maps

These maps change the color of the pixels in a material. Let's have a look:

### Color Correction Map

This map is allows you to modify color of a map using various tools. This map uses a stack-based method.

### Output Map

You can use this map to apply output settings to the procedural maps such as **Checker** or **Marble**. These maps don't have the output settings.

### RGB Tint Map

This map adjusts the three color channels in an image.

### Vertex Color Map

In 3ds Max, you can assign vertex colors using the **VertexPaint** modifier, the **Assign Vertex Colors** utility, or the vertex controls for an editable mesh, editable patch, or editable poly. This map makes any vertex coloring applied to an object available for rendering.

## Reflection and Refraction Maps

These maps are used to create reflections and refractions. Here's is a quick rundown.

### Flat Mirror Map

This map produces a material that reflects surroundings when it is applied to the co-planer faces. It is assigned to the **Reflection** map of the material.

### Raytrace Map

This map allows you to create fully raytraced reflections and refractions. The reflections/refractions generated by this map are more accurate than the **Reflect/Refract** map.

### Reflect/Refract Map

You can use this map to create a reflective or refractive surface. To create reflection, assign this map type to the reflection map. To create refraction, apply it to the **Refraction** map.

### Thin Wall Refraction Map

This map can be used to simulate a surface as if it part of a surface through a plate of glass.

## Other Maps

In 2017 version of 3ds Max, Autodesk has introduced some new maps. Here's is a quick rundown.

### Shape Map

You can use this map to create resolution independent graphical textures that you can animate. This map uses splines to apply textures to the selected object. The results can be fully animated. You can set outlines, fill colors as well as the map boundaries. You can change the shape of the spline even after applying it to the object in the scene. Also, all adjustment to the shape can be keyframed as a result you can animate the textures. The functioning of this map is demonstrated in an hands-on exercise later in the unit.

### Text Map

Like splines, you can also create textures using text. You can create creative textures using the **Text** map and all adjustments can be animated. The functioning of this map is demonstrated in an hands-on exercise later in the unit.

### TextureObjMask

This texture map allows you to control the textures using a primitive control object [plane, box, or sphere]. You can use the box or sphere primitive to control inside/outside color. The plan primitive allows you to control above/below color. The functioning of this map is demonstrated in an hands-on exercise later in the unit.

### Color Map

This map allows you to create solid color swatches and bitmaps. You can easily create and instance solid color swatches that allows you to maintain consistency and accuracy of color choices. You can also use a bitmap as an input and adjust gamma and gain.

### Combustion

You can use this map to interactively create maps using Autodesk Combustion and 3ds Max simultaneously. When you paint a map in combustion the material automatically updated in 3ds Max [material editor and shaded viewports].

*Caution: Combustion*
*This map works only if Autodesk Combustion is installed on your system. 3ds Max is only available for Windows, as a result, you can not use this map on a Macintosh system.*

### Map Output Selector

This map is used with the multi-output map such as Substance. It tells 3ds Max which output to use. This map is automatically inserted when you assign an output of multi-output Substance map to input of a material.

### MultiTile

This texture allows you to implement support for UDIM, Z-Brush, and Mudbox compaitble multi-tile textures. ZBrush is the default value.

# Hands-on Exercises

From the **Application** menu, choose **Manage | Set Project Folder** to open the **Browse for Folder** dialog. Navigate to the folder where you want to save the files and then click **Make New Folder**. Create the new folder with the name **unit-mt2** and click **OK** to create the project directory.

## Exercise 1: Creating the Gold Material

In this exercise, we are going to create the gold material.

The following table summarizes the exercise.

| **Table E1:** Creating the gold material | |
| --- | --- |
| Topics in this section: | • Getting Ready<br>• Creating the Gold Material |
| Skill Level | Beginner |
| Project Folder | **unit-mt2** |
| Start File | **umt2-hoe1-1to13-start.max** |
| Final Exercise File | **umt2-hoe1-end.max** |
| Time to Complete | 10 Minutes |

### Getting Ready

Open the **umt2-hoe1-1to13-start.max** file in 3ds Max.

### Creating the Gold Material

Press M to open the **Slate Material Editor**. On the **Material/Map Browser | Materials | General** rollout, drag the **Standard** material to the active view. Rename the material as **goldMat**. Apply the material to **geo1**, **geo2**, and **geo3**. Save the scene as **umt2-hoe1-end.max**. On the **Parameter Editor | goldMat | Shader Basic Parameters** rollout, choose **Multi-Layer** from the drop-down. On the **Multi-Layer Basic Parameters** rollout, set **Diffuse** to **RGB [148, 70, 0]** and then set **Diffuse Level** to **25**. Take a test render [see Figure E1].

Now, we will add specularity and reflection to add the detail. On the **First Specular Layer** section, set **Color** to **RGB [247, 227, 10]**. Set **Level** to **114**, **Glossiness** to **32**, **Anisotropy** to **82**, and **Orientation** to **90**. On the **Second Specular Layer** section, set **Color** to **RGB [192, 77, 8]**. Set **Level** to **114**, **Glossiness** to **32**, **Anisotropy** to **82**, and **Orientation** to **90**. On the **Maps** rollout, click **Reflection** map button. On the **Material/Map Browser** that appears, double-click **Falloff**.

On the **Parameter Editor | Falloff | Falloff Parameters** rollout, click the **Swap Color/Maps** button. Also, set **Falloff Type** to **Fresnel**. Click white swatch map button and then on the **Material/Map Browser** that appears, double-click **Raytrace** in the **General** rollout. On the **Parameter Editor | Raytrace | Raytracer Parameters** rollout, select **Reflection** from the **Trace Mode** section. Take a test render [see Figure E2].

On the **Falloff | Mix Curve** rollout, RMB click on the first point and then choose **Bezier-Corner** from the contextual menu [see Figure E3]. Similarly, convert second point to **Bezier-Corner** and change the shape of the curve as shown in Figure E4. Now, take a render to view the final result [see Figure E5].

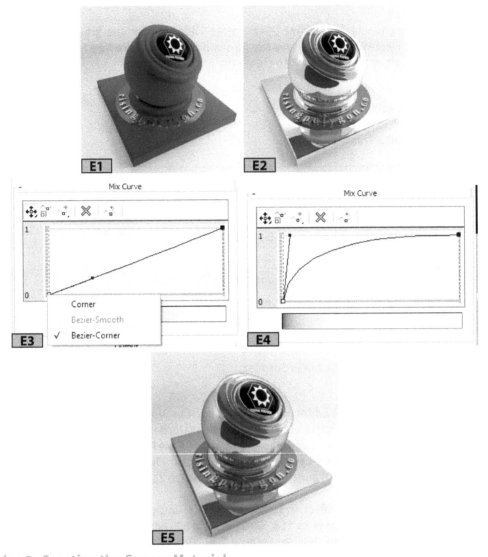

## Exercise 2: Creating the Copper Material

In this exercise, we are going to create the copper material.

The following table summarizes the exercise.

| Table E2: Creating the copper material | |
|---|---|
| Topics in this section: | • Getting Ready<br>• Creating the Copper Material |
| Skill Level | Beginner |
| Project Folder | **unit-mt2** |

| Start File | **umt2-hoe1-end.max** |
|---|---|
| Final Exercise File | **umt2-hoe2-end.max** |
| Time to Complete | 10 Minutes |

### Getting Ready

Make sure the **umt2-hoe1-end.max** file that you created in Hands-on Exercise 1 is open in 3ds Max.

### Creating the Copper Material

Press M to open the **Slate Material Editor**, if not already open. Create a copy of the **goldMat** node by shift dragging it [see Figure E1].

Rename the node as **copperMat** and then apply it to **geo1**, **geo2**, and **geo3**. Save the scene as **umt2-hoe2-end.max**.

On the **Multi-Layer Basic Parameters** rollout, set **Diffuse** to **RGB [88, 28, 9]**. On the **First Specular Layer section**, set **Color** to **RGB [177, 75, 44]**.

On the **Second Specular Layer section**, set **Color** to **RGB [255, 123, 82]**. Take the render [see Figure E2].

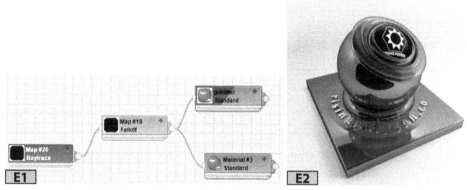

E1

E2

### Exercise 3: Creating the Brass Material

In this exercise, we are going to create the brass material.

The following table summarizes the exercise.

| **Table E3:** Creating the brass material | |
|---|---|
| Topics in this section: | • Getting Ready<br>• Creating the Brass Material |
| Skill Level | Beginner |
| Project Folder | **unit-mt2** |
| Start File | **umt2-hoe2-end.max** |
| Final Exercise File | **umt2-hoe3-end.max** |
| Time to Complete | 10 Minutes |

### Getting Ready

Make sure the **umt2-hoe2-end.max** file that you created in Hands-on Exercise 2 is open in 3ds Max.

### Creating the Brass Material

Press M to open the **Slate Material Editor**, if not already open. Create a copy of the **copperMat** node by **Shift** dragging it. Rename the node as **brassMat** and then apply it to **geo1**, **geo2**, and **geo3**.

On the **Multi-Layer Basic Parameters** rollout, set **Diffuse** to **RGB [49, 38, 14]**. On the **First Specular Layer** section, set **Color** to **RGB [212, 154, 30]**. On the **Second Specular Layer** section, set **Color** to **RGB [174, 98, 61]**. Take the render [see Figure E1] and then save the file with the name **umt2-hoe3-end.max**.

E1

### Exercise 4: Creating the Chrome Material

In this exercise, we are going to create the chrome material.

The following table summarizes the exercise.

| Table E4: Creating the chrome material | |
| --- | --- |
| Topics in this section: | • Getting Ready<br>• Creating the Chrome Material |
| Skill Level | Beginner |
| Project Folder | **unit-mt2** |
| Start File | **umt2-hoe1-1to13-start.max** |
| Final Exercise File | **umt2-hoes4-end.max** |
| Time to Complete | 10 Minutes |

### Getting Ready

Make sure the **hoes1-1to13-start.max** is open in 3ds Max.

### Creating the Chrome Material

Load **umt2-hoe1-1to13-start.max** in 3ds Max. Press **M** to open the **Slate Material Editor**. On the **Material/Map/Browser | Materials | General** rollout, drag the **Standard** material to the active view. Rename the material as **chromeMat**. Apply the material to **geo1**, **geo2**, and **geo3**. Save the scene as **umt2-hoes4-end.max**.

On the **Parameter Editor | chromeMat | Blinn Basic Parameters** rollout, click the **Diffuse** color swatch. On the **Color Selector : Diffuse Color** dialog, set **Value** to **12** and click **OK**. On the **Specular Highlights** section, set **Specular Level** to **150** and **Glossiness** to **80**.

E1

On the **Maps** rollout, set **Reflection** to **90** and then click the **Reflection** map button. On the **Material Map Browser** that appears, double-click **Raytrace**. On the **Raytrace** map | **Raytracer Parameters** | **Background** section, click **None**. On the **Material/Map Browser** that appears, double-click **Bitmap**. In the **Select Bitmap Image File** dialog that appears, select **refMap.jpeg**. Render the scene [see Figure E1].

## Exercise 5: Creating the Brushed Aluminum Material

In this exercise, we are going to create the brushed aluminum material using Photoshop and 3ds Max. The following table summarizes the exercise.

| **Table E5:** Creating the brushed aluminum material | |
|---|---|
| Topics in this section: | • Getting Ready<br>• Creating the Brushed Aluminum Material |
| Skill Level | Beginner |
| Project Folder | **unit-mt2** |
| Start File | **umt2-hoe1-1to13-start.max** |
| Final Exercise File | **umt2-hoe5-end.max** |
| Time to Complete | 15 Minutes |

### Getting Ready

Make sure the **umt2-hoe1-1to13-start.max** is open in 3ds Max.

### Creating the Brushed Aluminum Material

Start Photoshop. Create a **1000 x 1000 px** document and fill it with **50%** gray color. Choose **Noise | Add Noise** from the **Filter** menu and then set the parameters as shown in Figure E1 and then click **OK**. Choose **Blur | Motion Blur** from the **Filter** menu and then set the parameters as shown in Figure E2 and then click **OK**.

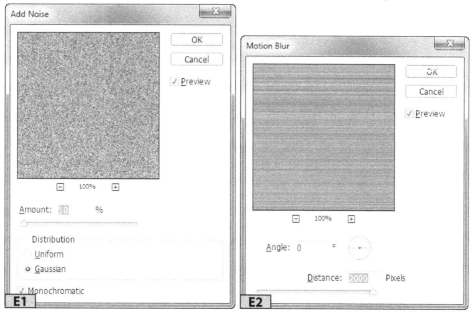

Choose **Adjustments | Brightness\Contrast** from the **Image** menu and then set the parameters as shown in Figure E3 and then click **OK**. Save the document as **scratch.jpg**.

Load **umt2-hoe1-1to13-start.max** in 3ds Max, if not already loaded. Press **M** to open the **Slate Material Editor**. On the **Material/Map Browser | Materials | General** rollout, drag the **Standard** material to the active view. Rename the material as **balMat**. Apply the material to **geo1**, **geo2**, and **geo3**.

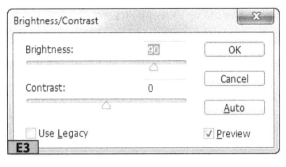

On the **Parameter Editor | balMat | Shader Basic Parameters** rollout, choose **Oren-Nayar-Blinn** from the drop-down. On the **Parameter Editor | balMat | Oren-Nayar-Blinn Basic Parameters** rollout, click **Ambient** color swatch. On the **Color Selector : Ambient Color** dialog, set **Value** to **84** and click **OK**. Unlock the **Ambient** and **Diffuse** components of the material.

Click the **Diffuse** map button and then on the **Material/Map Browser** that appears, double-click **Mix**. On the **Parameter Editor | Mix map**, set **Color 1** to **127** and assign **scratch.jpg** to **Color 2** using the **Bitmap** map. Set **Mix** Amount to **72%**. On the **balMat | Oren-Nayar-Blinn Basic Parameters** rollout | **Advanced Diffuse** section, set **Diffuse Level** to **81**, and **Roughness** to **80**. Now, take a test render [see Figure E4].

On the **Parameter Editor | balMat | Oren-Nayar-Blinn Basic Parameters** rollout | **Specular Highlight** section, set **Specular Level** to **156**, **Glossiness** to **13**, and **Soften** to **0.48**. Now, take a test render [see Figure E5]. On the **Parameter Editor | scratch.jpg | Output** rollout, set **Output Amount** to **0.6**. Take a render [see Figure E6]. Save the file as **umt2-hoe5-end.max**.

Exercise 6: Creating the Denim Fabric Material

In this exercise, we are going to create the denim fabric material using Photoshop and 3ds Max.

The following table summarizes the exercise.

| **Table E6:** Creating the denim fabric material | |
|---|---|
| Topics in this section: | • Getting Ready<br>• Creating the Denim Fabric Material |
| Skill Level | Beginner |

| Project Folder | unit-mt2 |
|---|---|
| Start File | umt2-hoe1-1to13-start.max |
| Final Exercise File | umt2-hoe6-end.max |
| Time to Complete | 15 Minutes |

## Getting Ready
Make sure the **umt2-hoe1-1to13-start.max** is open in 3ds Max.

## Creating the Denim Fabric Material
Start Photoshop. Create a **1000 x 1000 px** document and fill it with **RGB [41, 67, 102]** color. Create a new layer and fill it with **50%** gray. Press **D** to switch to the default colors. Choose **Filter Gallery| Sketch | Halftone Pattern** from the **Filter** menu and then set the parameters as shown in Figure E1 and then click **OK**. Choose **Pixelate | Mezzotint** from the **Filter** menu and then set the parameters as shown in Figure E2 and then click **OK**.

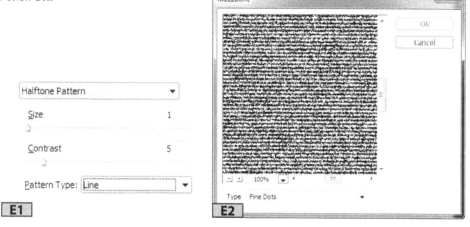

Duplicate the layer and rotate and scale the duplicate layer [see Figure E3]. Choose **Blur | Gaussian Blur** from the **Filter** menu and then apply a blur of radius **1**. Set blending mode to **Multiply**. Also, set the blending mode of the middle layer [Layer 1] to **Softlight** [Figure E4].

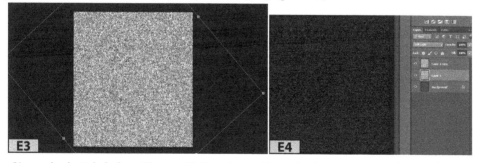

Save the file as **denimFebric.jpg**. Choose **Flatten Image** from the **Layer** menu to flatten the image. Now, press **Ctrl+Shift+U** to desaturate the image and then save it as **denimFebricBump.jpg**. In 3ds Max, press **M** to open the **Slate Material Editor**. On the **Material/Map Browser | Materials | Scanline** rollout, drag the **Standard** material to the active view. Rename the material as **denimMat**. Apply the material to **geo1**, **geo2**, and **geo3**.

Save the scene as **umt2-hoe6-end.max**. On the **Parameter Editor | denimMat | Shader Basic Parameters** rollout, choose **Oren-Nayar-Blinn** from the drop-down. On the **Parameter Editor | denimMat | Oren-Nayar-Blinn Basic Parameters** rollout, click **Ambient** color swatch.

On the **Color Selector : Ambient Color** dialog, set **RGB** to **50**, **53**, and **57** and click **OK**. Unlock the **Ambient** and **Diffuse** components of the material. Click the **Diffuse** map button and then on the **Material Map Browser** that appears, double-click **Bitmap**. Assign **denimFebric.jpg**. On the **denimMat | Oren-Nayar-Blinn Basic Parameters** rollout | **Advanced Diffuse** section, set **Diffuse Level** to **250**, and **Roughness** to **75**. Now, take a test render [see Figure E5].

On the **Parameter Editor | denimMat | Oren-Nayar-Blinn Basic Parameters** rollout | **Specular Highlight** section, set **Specular Level** to **7**, and **Glossiness** to **10**. Take a test render [see Figure E6]. On the **Maps** rollout, ensure **Bump** is set to **30%** and then click **Bump** map button.

On the **Material/Map Browser** that appears, double-click **Bitmap**. On the **Select Bitmap Image File** dialog that appears, select **denimFebricBump.jpg**. Take a test render [see Figure E7].

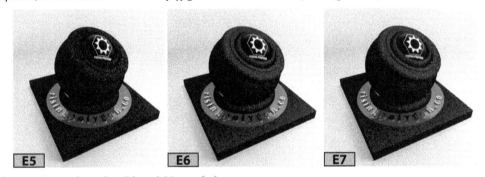

| E5 | E6 | E7 |

## Exercise 7: Creating the Blend Material
In this exercise, we are going to create a blend material.

The following table summarizes the exercise.

| **Table E7:** Working with the blend material | |
| --- | --- |
| Topics in this section: | •    Getting Ready<br>•    Working with the Blend Material |
| Skill Level | Beginner |
| Project Folder | **unit-mt2** |
| Start File | **umt2-hoe1-1to13-start.max** |
| Final Exercise File | **umt2-hoe7-end.max** |
| Time to Complete | 15 Minutes |

### Getting Ready
Make sure the **umt2-hoe1-1to13-start.max** is open in 3ds Max.

## Working with the Blend Material

Save the scene as **umt2-hoe7-end.max**. Press **M** to open the **Slate Material Editor**. On the **Material/Map Browser | Materials | General** rollout, drag the **Blend** material to the active view. Rename the materials connected to the **Blend** node as **mat1** and **mat2**. Apply the **Blend** material to **geo1**, **geo2**, and **geo3**.

Assign **ConcreteBare.jpg** to the **mat1 | Diffuse** map and **ConcreteBare1.jpg** to the **mat2 | Diffuse** map. Take a test render [see Figure E1]. Assign a **Noise** map to the **Blend** material's **Mask** control. On the **Mixing Curve** section, turn on the **Use Curve** switch and set **Upper** to **0.78** and **Lower** to **0.3**. Take a test render [see Figure E2].

On the **Parameter Editor | Noise Parameters** rollout, set **Noise Type** to **Fractal**, **High** to **0.9**, and **Size** to **15.5**. Take a test render and press **Ctrl+S** to save the file. For the sake of clarity, I have rendered [see Figure E3] a plane with **mat1** (left image), **mat2** (middle image), and **Blend** (right image) materials applied. Figure E4 shows the node network.

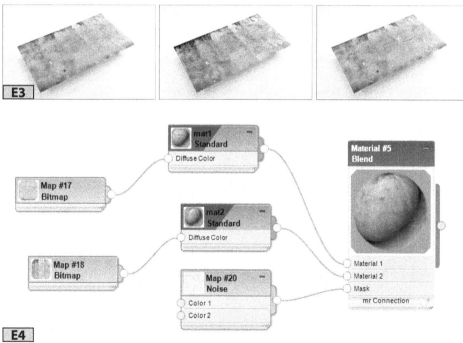

In this exercise, we are going to create a double-sided material.

The following table summarizes the exercise.

| Table E8: Working with the double-sided material | |
|---|---|
| Topics in this section: | • Getting Ready<br>• Working with the Double-Sided Material |
| Skill Level | Beginner |
| Project Folder | **unit-mt2** |
| Start File | **umt2-hoe1-1to13-start.max** |
| Final Exercise File | **umt2-hoe8-end.max** |
| Time to Complete | 15 Minutes |

Getting Ready

Make sure the **umt2-hoe1-1to13-start.max** is open in 3ds Max. Save file as **umt2-hoe8-end.max**.

Working with the Double Sided Material

Delete **geo4**, **geo1**, **geo6** from the scene and place a teapot at the center of **geo5**. Go to the **Modify** panel and then on the **Parameters** rollout | **Teapot Parts** section, turn off **Handle**, **Spout**, and **Lid** switches. Also, set **Segments** to **32**.

Press **M** to open the **Slate Material Editor**. On the **Material/Map Browser** | **Materials** | **General** rollout, drag the **Double Sided** material to the active view. Rename the materials connected to the **DoubleSided** node as **mat1** and **mat2**. Apply the material to the teapot.

Now, we will assign maps to the back and facing materials of the **Double Sided** material. The **Facing Material** is represented by **mat1** whereas the **Back Material** is represented by **mat2**.

Assign **ConcreteBare.jpg** to the **mat1** | **Diffuse** map. Assign a **Perlin Marble** map to the **mat2** | **Diffuse** map. Set **Translucency** to **25** in the **Double Sided** material | **Double Sided Basic Parameters** rollout. Take a test render [see Figure E1] and press **Ctrl+S** to save the file. Figure E2 shows the node network.

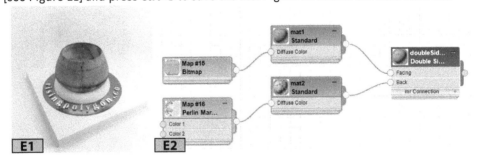

In this exercise, we are going to create a **Shellac** material.

The following table summarizes the exercise.

| **Table E9:** Working with the **Shellac** material | |
|---|---|
| Topics in this section: | • Getting Ready<br>• Working with the **Shellac** Material |
| Skill Level | Beginner |
| Project Folder | **unit-mt2** |
| Start File | **umt2-hoe8-end.max** |
| Final Exercise File | **umt2-hoe9-end.max** |
| Time to Complete | 15 Minutes |

Getting Ready

Make sure the **umt2-hoe8-end.max** is open in 3ds Max. Save it as **umt2-hoe9-end.max**. Turn on the **Lid** for the teapot.

Working with the Shellác Material

Press **M** to open the **Slate Material Editor**. On the **Material/Map Browser | Materials | General** rollout, drag the **Shellac** material to the active view.

Rename the materials connected to the **Base Material** and **Shellac Mat** ports of the **Shellac** node as **mat1** and **mat2**, respectively. Apply the material to the teapot.

E1

Assign the **Swirl** map to the **mat1 | Diffuse** map and **Wood** map to the **mat2 | Diffuse** map. Set **Shellac Color Blend** to **86** in the **Shellac Basic Parameters** rollout. Take a test render [see Figure E1].

Exercise 10: Creating the Microscopic Material

In this exercise, we're going to create a microscopic material [see Figure E1]. The following material(s) and map(s) are used in this exercise: **Standard, Mix, Falloff**, and **Noise**.

The following table summarizes the exercise.

| **Table E10:** Creating the microscopic material | |
|---|---|
| Topics in this section: | • Getting Ready<br>• Creating the Microscopic Material |
| Skill Level | Beginner |
| Project Folder | **unit-mt2** |

| Start File | **umt2-hoe10-start.max** |
|---|---|
| Final Exercise File | **umt2-hoe10-end.max** |
| Time to Complete | 15 Minutes |

Getting Ready
Make sure the **umt2-hoe10-start.max** is open in 3ds Max.

Creating the Microscopic Material
Press **M** to open the **Slate Material Editor** and then create a new **Standard** material and assign it to the **sphGeo** in the scene. Rename the material as **msMat**. Connect a **Falloff** map to the **msMat's Diffuse** port. On the **Parameter Editor | Falloff** map | **Falloff Parameters** rollout | **Front:Side** section, set first color swatch to **RGB [20, 20, 20]** and second color swatch to white. Set **Falloff Type** to **Perpendicular/Parallel**. Ensure **Falloff Direction** is set to **Viewing Direction (Camera Z-Axis)** [see Figure E2]. Also, set the **Mix Curve** to as shown in Figure E3.

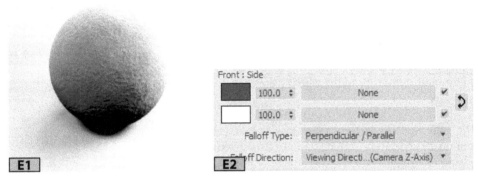

Now, you will create two **Noise** maps and mix them using the **Mix** map. Connect a **Mix** map to the **msMat's Bump** port. On the **Parameter Editor | Mix** map | **Mix Parameters** rollout, set **Mix Amount** to **37.8**. On the **Slate Material Editor**, connect two **Noise** maps, one each to the **Color 1** and **Color 2** ports. For the **Color 1 | Noise** map use the settings shown in Figure E4. Figure E5 shows the **Noise** map settings connected to **Color 2**. Figure E6 shows the node network.

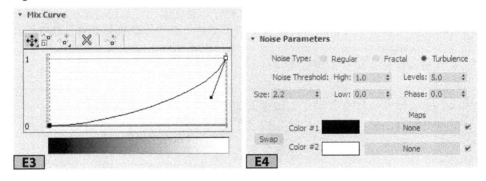

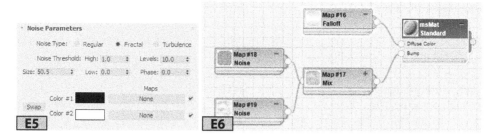

Now, render the scene. Notice that the output is little bit on the darker side. To address this, on the **Parameter Editor** | **Falloff** map | **Falloff Parameters** rollout | **Front:Side** section, set first color swatch to **RGB [80, 80, 80]**. Render the scene [see Figure E1].

## Exercise 11: Creating Material for a Volleyball

Here, we are going to apply texture to a volleyball [see Figure E1]. Right image in Figure E1 shows the reference whereas the left image shows the rendered output. The following material(s) and map(s) are used in this exercise: **Multi/Sub-Object**, **Standard**, and **Noise**.

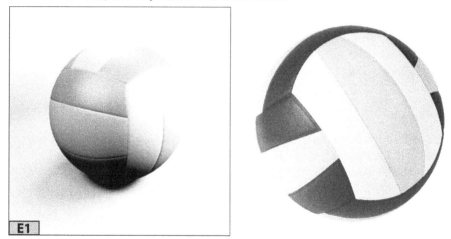

The following table summarizes the exercise.

| Table E11: Creating material for a volleyball | |
|---|---|
| Topics in this section: | • Getting Ready<br>• Creating Material for a Volleyball |
| Skill Level | Beginner |
| Project Folder | **unit-mt2** |
| Start File | **umt2-hoe11-start.max** |
| Final Exercise File | **umt2-hoe11-end.max** |
| Time to Complete | 15 Minutes |

### Getting Ready

Make sure the **umt2-hoe11-start.max** is open in 3ds Max. Save the file as **umt2-hoe11-end.max**.

## Creating Material for a Volleyball

Select the **VolleyBallGeo** in any viewport and then go to the **Modify** panel. On the **Selection** rollout, click **Element** and then select the elements that make the yellow part of the volleyball [see Figure E2]. See the right image in Figure E1 for reference.

On the **Modify panel | Polygon: Material IDs** rollout, set **ID** to **1** [see Figure E3]. Similarly, select the blue and white elements and assign them ID **2** and **3**, respectively. Press **M** to open the **Slate Material Editor** and then create a new **Multi/Sub-object** material and assign it to the **VolleyBallGeo** in the scene. Rename the material as **vbMat**. On the **Parameter Editor | vbMat | Multi/Sub-Object Parameters** rollout, click **Set Number** and then set **Number of Materials** to **3** in the dialog that appears. Next, click **OK**. In the **Slate Material Editor**, connect a **Standard** material to the port **1** of the **vbMat**. On the **Parameter Editor | Blinn Basic Parameter** rollout, set the **Diffuse** component to **RGB [242, 140, 8]**. On the **Specular Highlights** section, set **Specular Level** to **71** and **Glossiness** to **28**.

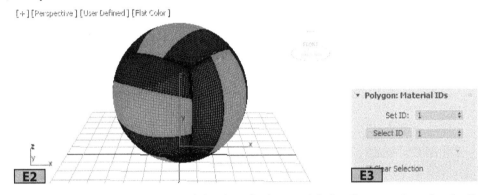

Connect a **Noise** map to the **Bump** port of the **Standard** material. Set **Bump** to **2%**. On the **Parameter Editor | Noise map | Noise Parameters** rollout, set **Noise Type** to **Turbulence**, **Levels** to **9**, and **Size** to **0.5**. On the **Slate Material Editor**, select the **Standard** material and **Noise** map. Now, create a copy of the selected nodes using **SHIFT**. Connect the new Standard material to the port **2** of the **vbMat**. Similarly, create another copy and connect it to port **3**. Figure E4 shows the node network. Set **Diffuse** components of the material connected to the port **2** and **3** to **RGB [11, 91, 229]** and **RGB [236, 236, 230]**, respectively. Now, press F9 to take a render.

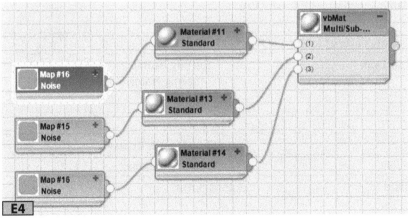

Here, we are going to apply texture to a water tunnel [see Figure E1]. The following material(s) and map(s) are used in this exercise: **Raytrace**, **Standard**, **Mix**, and **Noise**.

The following table summarizes the exercise.

| **Table E12:** Creating material for a water tunnel | |
| --- | --- |
| Topics in this section: | • Getting Ready<br>• Creating Material for a Water Tunnel |
| Skill Level | Beginner |
| Project Folder | **unit-mt2** |
| Start File | **umt2-hoes12-start.max** |
| Final Exercise File | **umt2-hoes12-end.max** |
| Time to Complete | 15 Minutes |

## Getting Ready

Make sure the **umt2-hoes12-start.max** is open in 3ds Max.

## Creating Material for a Water Tunnel

Press **M** to open the **Slate Material Editor** and then create a new **Raytrace** material and assign it to the **waterGeo** in the scene. Rename the material as **waterMat**. On the **Parameter Editor | Raytrace Basic Parameter** rollout, set **Diffuse** to black. Set **Transparency** to **RGB (146, 175, 223)**. Set **Reflect** to **RGB [178, 178, 178]**. On the **Specular Highlight** section, set **Specular Level** to **161** and **Glossiness** to **29**. Connect a **Noise** map to the **Bump** port of the **waterMat**. Use the default values for the **Noise** map. Press **F9** to render the scene [Figure E2].

On the **Slate Material Editor**, create a new **Standard** material and assign it to the **caveGeo** in the scene. Rename the material as **caveMat**. Connect a **Mix** map to the **Diffuse** port of the **caveMat**. Connect a **Noise** map to the **Color 1** port of the **Mix** map. On the **Noise Parameters** rollout, set **Noise Type** to **Turbulence**, **Levels** to **10**, **Size** to **31.7**. Set **Color 1** to **RGB [132, 77, 6]** and **Color 2** to **RGB [154, 100, 79]**. Connect a **Noise** map to the **Color 2** port of the **Mix** map. On the **Noise Parameters** rollout, set **Noise Type** to **Turbulence**, **Levels** to **10**, **Size** to **72**. Set **Color 1** to **RGB [212, 84, 45]** and **Color 2** to **RGB [181, 99, 54]**.

On the **Parameter Editor | Mix Parameters** rollout, set **Mix Amount** to **40**. On the **Mixing curve** section, turn on the **Use Curve** switch and then set **Upper** to **0.6** and **Lower** to **0.53**. Take a test render [Figure E3].

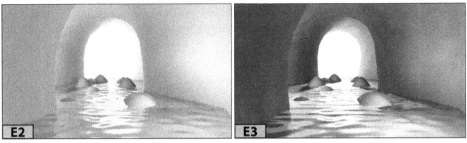

Connect a **Mix** map to the **Displacement** port of the **caveMat**. Set **Displacement** to **25%**. Connect a **Noise** map to the **Color 1** port of the **Mix** map. On the **Noise Parameters** rollout, set **Noise Type** to **Turbulence**, **Levels** to **8.4**, **Size** to **21.2**. Connect a **Noise** map to the **Color 2** port of the **Mix** map. On the **Noise Parameters** rollout, set **Noise Type** to **Turbulence**, **Levels** to **10**, **Size** to **81.5**. On the **Parameter Editor | Mix Parameters** rollout, set **Mix Amount** to **18.4**. Take a test render [Figure E4].

Similarly, create a material for the **floorGeo**. If you want to see the values I have used, open **umt2-hoe12-end.max** and check the **floorMat** material.

### Exercise 13: Creating Rusted Metal Texture

Let's now create a rusted metal texture [see Figure E1]. The following material(s) and map(s) are used in this exercise: **Standard**, **Composite**, **Bitmap**, **Color Correction**, and **Noise**. The following table summarizes the exercise.

| **Table E13:** Creating rusted metal texture | |
| --- | --- |
| Topics in this section: | • Getting Ready<br>• Creating Rusted Metal Texture |
| Skill Level | Beginner |
| Project Folder | **unit-mt2** |
| Start File | **umt2-hoe1-1to13-start.max** |
| Final Exercise File | **umt2-hoe13-end.max** |
| Time to Complete | 15 Minutes |

## Getting Ready

Make sure the **umt2-hoe1-1to13-start.max** is open in 3ds Max. Save the file with the name **umt2-hoe13-end.max**.

## Creating Rusted Metal Texture

Press **M** to open the **Slate Material Editor**. In the **Material/Map Browser | Materials | General** rollout, double-click on **Standard** to add a **Standard** material to the active view. Rename the material as **rustMat** and apply it to **geo1**, **geo2**, and **geo3**.

In the **Parameter Editor | Shader Basic Parameters** rollout, turn on the **2-Sided** switch. Connect a **Composite** map to the **rustMap's Diffuse Color** port. Now, connect **rust.jpg** to the **Composite** map's **Layer 1** port [see Figure E2].

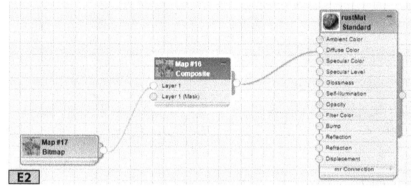

On the **Parameter Editor | Composite** map | **Composite Layers | Layer 1** rollout, click **Add a New Layer** button to add a new layer [see Figure E3]. Notice that a new port with the name **Layer 2** has been added to the **Composite** map node in the active view. Connect **rustPaint.jpg** to the **Composite** map's **Layer 2** port. On the **Parameter Editor | Composite** map | **Composite Layers | Layer 2** rollout, set **Opacity** to **10%** and blend mode to **Color Dodge** [see Figure E4].

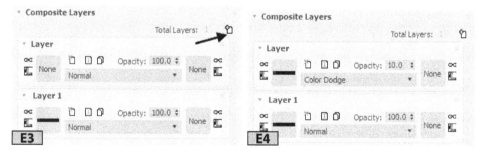

Now, take a test render [see Figure E5]. Connect **scratchesMask.jpg** to the **Composite** map's **Layer 2 (Mask)** port using a **Bitmap** map. Now, check the **Invert** checkbox from the **Bitmap's Output** rollout. Take a test render [see Figure E6]. On the **Slate Material Editor's** active view, create copy of the **Bitmap** node connected to the **Composite** map's **Layer 2 (Mask)** node using **Shift**. Connect the duplicate node to the **Bump** node of **rustMat**. On the **Parameter Editor | rustMat | Maps** rollout, set bump map's strength to **10%** and then take a test render [see Figure E7].

E5     E6     E7

## Exercise 14: Shading an outdoor Scene

In this exercise, we are going to apply materials and textures to an outdoor scene [see Figure E1]. The following table summarizes the exercise.

E1

| Table E14: Shading an outdoor scene | |
|---|---|
| In this exercise, you will: | • Apply material to the objects<br>• Use the **UVW Map** modifier<br>• Apply textures to the material |
| Topics in this section: | • Getting Ready<br>• Shading the Scene |
| Skill Level | Intermediate |
| Project Folder | **unit-mt2** |
| Start File | **umt2-hoe14-start.max** |
| Final Exercise File | **umt2-hoe14-end.max** |
| Time to Complete | 30 Minutes |

### Getting Ready

Make sure the **umt2-hoe14-start.max** is open in 3ds Max. Save the file with the name **umt2-hoe14-end.max**.

### Shading the Scene

Select **wallGeo** from the **Scene Explorer** and then press **M** to open the **Slate Material Editor**. Drag **Standard** from the **Material/Map Browser | Maps | Scanline** rollout to the **Active View**. Rename the material as **wallMat**. RMB click on the **wallMat** node and then choose **Assign Material to Selection**. Again, RMB click and then choose **Show Shaded Material in Viewport**.

In the **Active View**, drag the **Diffuse Color** socket onto the empty area and release the mouse button. Choose **General | Bitmap** from the popup menu. In the **Select Bitmap Image File** dialog that opens, select **redBrick.png** and then click **Open** to make a connection between the **Diffuse Color** socket and texture. Double-click on the **Bitmap** node and then in the **Parameter Editor | Coordinates** rollout, set **U Tiling** and **V Tiling** to **4**. Similarly, connect the **Bump** socket to the **redBrickGray.png** and set **Tiling** to **4**.

Notice in the viewport the map is displayed on the wall [see the left image in Figure E2]. Ensure **wallGeo** is selected in the **Scene Explorer** and then go to **Modify** panel and add the **UVW Map** modifier to the stack. Select the modifier's **Gizmo** and scale the texture so that the size of the bricks appear in right proportions [see the right image in Figure E2].

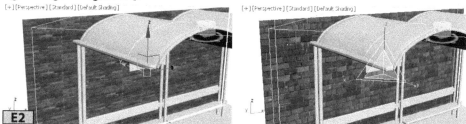

Select **floorGeo** from the **Scene Explorer** and then in the **Slate Material Editor**, drag **Standard** from the **Material/Map Browser | Maps | General** rollout to the **Active View**. Rename the material as **roadMat**. RMB click on the **roadMat** node and then choose **Assign Material to Selection**. Again, RMB click and then choose **Show Shaded Material in Viewport**. In the **Active View**, drag the **Diffuse Color** socket onto the empty area and release the mouse button. Choose **General | Bitmap** from the popup menu. In the **Select Bitmap Image File** dialog that opens, select **road.jpg** and then click **Open** to make a connection between the **Diffuse Color** socket and texture. Notice in the viewport, the texture appears on the **floorGeo** [see Figure E3]. Now, we need to change the direction of the yellow line. We will do so by using the **UVW Map** modifier.

Ensure **floorGeo** is selected in the **Scene Explorer** and then go to **Modify** panel and add the **UVW Map** modifier to the stack. Select the modifier's **Gizmo** and rotate it by **90** degrees by using the **Rotate** tool. You can also use the **Move** tool to position the texture on the geometry [see Figure E4].

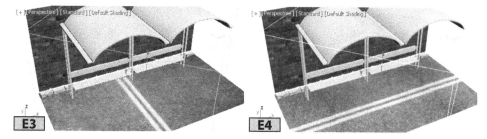

Now, we will apply the material to billboard. We will use the **Multi/Subobject** material. The ID **1** has been assigned to the screen component of the board whereas rest of the geometry is held by ID **2**. Select **billBoardGeo** from the **Scene Explorer** and then add a **Multi/Subobject** node to the **Active View**. Rename the material as **billboardMat**. In the **Parameter Editor**, click **Set Number**. Now, in the **Set Number of Materials** dialog, set **Number of Materials** field to **2** and click **OK**. RMB click on the **billboardMat** node and then choose **Assign Material to Selection**.

Drag the **1** socket to the empty area of the view and then choose **Materials | Scanline | Standard** from the popup menu. Connect the **Standard's** materials **Diffuse Color** socket to the **honda.jpg**. Connect another **Standard** material to the **2** socket of the **billboardMat**. In the **Parameter Editor | Blinn Basic Parameters rollout | Specular Highlight** group of the **Standard** material, set **Specular Level** and **Glossiness** to **92** and **33**, respectively. Also, set **Diffuse** color to **RGB [20, 20, and 20]**. The material appears on the **billBoardGeo** in the viewport [see Figure E5]. You need to enable **Show Shaded Material in Viewport** for the two Standard materials. Create two **Standard** materials and assign dark gray and yellow colors to them. Now, apply these materials to alternate brick from the **brickGrp** group [see Figure E6].

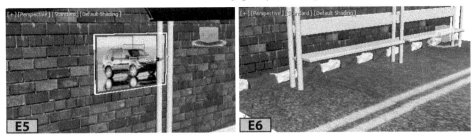

Now, create a chrome material as done in Exercise 4. Do not assign the **refMap.jpg** to the **Raytrace** map. In the **Scene Explorer**, select **bsGeo11, bsGeo12, bsGeo15, bsGeo16, bsGeo18, bsGeo19, bsGeo20, bsGeo22, bsGeo23, bsGeo24, bsGeo26,** and **bsGeo27**. Assign chrome material to the selected objects [see Figure E7]. Also, assign chrome material to **bsGeo3**, and **bsGeo6**.

In the **Scene Explorer**, select **bsGeo04, bsGeo05, bsGeo07,** and **bsGeo08**. Drag **Standard** from the **Material/ Map Browser | Maps | General** rollout to the **Active View**. Rename the material as **woodMat**. RMB click on the **woodMat** node and then choose **Assign Material to Selection**. Again, RMB click and then choose **Show Shaded Material in Viewport**. In the **Active View**, drag the **Diffuse Color** socket onto the empty area and release the mouse button. Choose **General | Wood** from the popup menu. In the **Parameter Editor | Wood | Wood Parameters** rollout, change **Color #2** to **RGB[106, 25, 0]**. The wood texture is displayed in the viewport [see Figure E8].

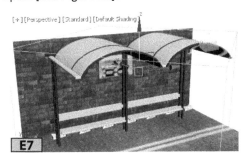 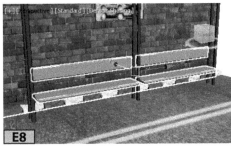

In the **Scene Explorer**, select **bsGeo21**, and **bsGeo25** and then drag **Standard** from the **Material/Map Browser | Maps | General** rollout to the **Active View**. Rename the material as **roofMat**. RMB click on the **roofMat** node and then choose **Assign Material to Selection**. Again, RMB click and then choose **Show Shaded Material in Viewport**. In the **Parameter Editor | roofMat | Blinn Basic Parameters** rollout, change **Diffuse** to **RGB[23, 241, 12]** and then set **Opacity** to **25**. Figure E9 shows the roof material in the viewport.

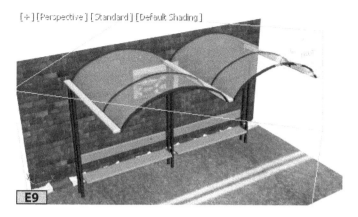

[+] [Perspective] [Standard] [Default Shading]

E9

## Exercise 15: Texturing a Cardboard Box

Let's start by texturing a cardboard box [see Figure E1] using the **UV Editor**.

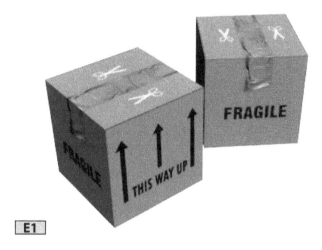

E1

The following Table summarizes the exercise.

| Table E15: Texturing a cardboard texture | |
|---|---|
| Topics in this section: | • Getting Ready<br>• Texturing the Cardboard Box |
| Skill Level | Intermediate |
| Project Folder | **unit-mt2** |
| Final Exercise File | **umt2-hoe15-end.max** |
| Time to Complete | 20 Minutes |

### Getting Ready

Reset 3ds Max. Set units to **Generic Units** and then create a box with the **Length**, **Height**, and **Width** set to **190**.

## Texturing the Cardboard Box

Ensure the box is selected in a viewport and then go to **Modify** panel. Add the **Unwrap UVW** modifier to the stack. Click **Polygon** on the **Selection** panel and then press **Ctrl+A** to select all polygons. On the **Projection** rollout, click **Box Map** and then click again to deactivate. On the **Edit UVs** rollout, click **Open UV Editor** to open the **Edit UVWs** window. Choose **Unfold Mapping** from the **Mapping** menu of the window. The **Unfold Mapping** dialog appears. Click **OK** to accept the default settings and unfold UVs [see Figure E2].

Choose **Pick Texture** from the drop-down located on the top-right corner of the window, the **Material/Map Browser** appears. In the browser, double-click on **Bitmap** from the **Maps | General** rollout. In the **Select Bitmap Image File** dialog, select **cardboard_texture.png** and click **Open**. The **cardboard_texture.png** appears in the **Edit UVWs** window [see Figure E3].

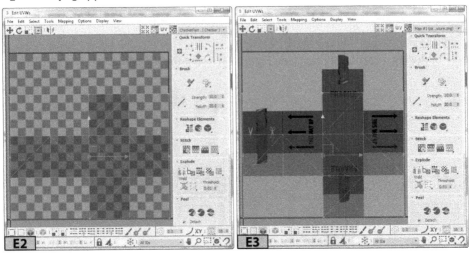

Click **Vertex** from the bottom-left corner of the window to activate the **Vertex** selection mode. All the vertices are selected. If they are not selected, press **Ctrl+A** to select them. Ensure **Move Selected Subobjects** is active from the window's toolbar and then align all UVs to the background texture [see Figure E4]. Press and hold **Shift** while dragging to constrain the movement.

Now, select a complete column of row of the vertices and align them with the background texture [see Figure E5]. You can also select vertices in a viewport. If the UVs are not in the straight line, you can use **Align Horizontally to Pivot** and **Align Vertically to Pivot** from the **Quick Transform** rollout of the window to straighten the UVs. Close the Edit UVWs window.

Press **M** to open the **Slate Material Editor**. From the **Material/Map Browser | Material** rollout | **Scanline** rollout, double-click **Standard** to add it to the **Active View** and then assign it to the box in the scene. Rename the material as **boxMat**. Connect **ardboard_texture.png** texture to the **Diffuse** slot of the material. RMB click on **boxMat** node and choose **Show Shaded Material in Viewport** from the menu to display the texture in the viewport.

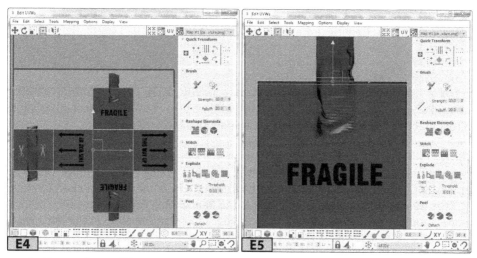

## Exercise 16: Texturing a Dice

Let's start by texturing a dice [see Figure E1] using the **UV Editor**. In this Exercise we will export the UVs template to the Photoshop and then use Photoshop to create the texture. We will then import the texture back into 3ds Max and will apply it to the dice geometry.

E1

The following Table summarizes the exercise.

| Table E16: Texturing a dice | |
|---|---|
| Topics in this section: | Getting Ready<br>Texturing a Dice |
| Skill Level | Intermediate |
| Project Folder | **unit-mt2** |
| Final Exercise File | **umt2-hoe16-end.max** |
| Time to Complete | 20 Minutes |

## Getting Ready

Reset 3ds Max. Set units to **Generic Units** and then create a box with the **Length**, **Height**, and **Width** set to **190**.

## Texturing the Dice

Ensure the box is selected in a viewport and then go to **Modify** panel. Add the **Unwrap UVW** modifier to the stack. Click **Polygon** 🔲 on the **Selection** panel and then press **Ctrl+A** to select all polygons. On the **Projection** rollout, click **Box Map** 🔲 and then click again to deactivate.

On the **Edit UVs** rollout, click **Open UV Editor** to open the **Edit UVWs** window. Choose **Unfold Mapping** from the **Mapping** menu of the window. The **Unfold Mapping** dialog appears. Click **OK** to accept the default settings and unfold UVs. Choose **Render UV Template** from the **Tools** menu to open the **Render UVs** dialog. Click **Render UV Template** on the dialog. The **Render Map** window appears. Click **Save Image** on the window's toolbar to open the **Save Image** dialog. Type **dice_template** in the **File name** field and choose **PNG Image File** from the **Save as** type drop-down.

Click **Save** to save the template. Click **OK** from the **PNG Configuration** dialog. Now, close all windows and dialogs, if open. Open **dice_template.png** in **Photoshop**. **Layer 0** appears in the **Layers** panel. Create a new layer below **Layer 0** and fill it with **black** [see Figure E2].

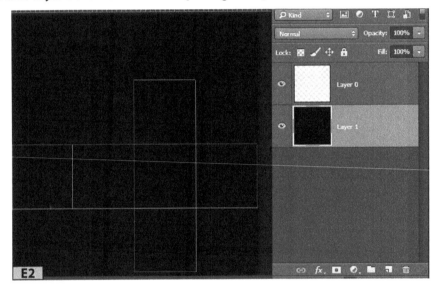

Now, using **Photoshop** tools and features create dice texture according to the dice template. I am putting simple numbers to identify the faces of the dice [see Figure E3]. You should go ahead and create a nice looking dice texture for your dice model.

Now, switch off the **black** layer and the **template** layer. Save the **Photoshop** document as **dice_texture.png**.

In 3ds Max, apply a **Standard** material to the box. Set **Diffuse color** to **red**. Connect **dice_texture.png** to the **Diffuse Color** and **Opacity** slots of the material's node, respectively. In the **dice_texture.png** map | **Bitmap Parameters** rollout, turn off the **Premultiplied Alpha** switch. Render the scene.

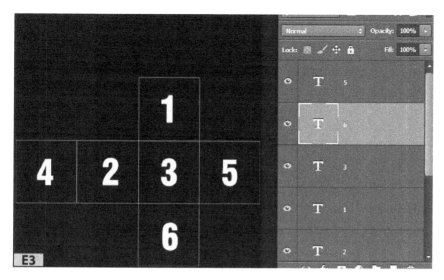

## Exercise 17: Texturing a Dice - II

In this Exercise, we will use an alternate method to texture a dice. You will use six different maps for the six faces of the dice.

The following Table summarizes the exercise.

| **Table E17**: Texturing a dice - II | |
|---|---|
| Topics in this section: | • Getting Ready<br>• Texturing a Dice |
| Skill Level | Intermediate |
| Project Folder | **unit-mt2** |
| Final Exercise File | **umt2-hoe17-end.max** |
| Time to Complete | 20 Minutes |

### Getting Ready

Reset 3ds Max. Set units to **Generic Units** and then create a box with the **Length**, **Height**, and **Width** set to **90**.

### Texturing the Dice

Ensure the box is selected in a viewport and add the **UVW Map** modifier to the stack. Select **Box** in the **Mapping** group of the **Parameters** rollout. Click **Fit** on the **Alignment** group. RMB click on the box in a viewport and then choose **Convert To : Convert to Editable Poly** from the **Quad** menu.

Press **M** to open the **Slate Material Editor** and then from the **Material/Map Browser | General | Maps** rollout, drag **Standard** to the active view. Connect **side-1.jpg** to the **Diffuse** slot of the material. Similarly, add **5** more **Standard** maps and assign **side-2.jpg** to **side-6.jpg** to them. RMB click on the **Standard** material nodes and then choose **Show Shaded Material in Viewport** from the menu.

Now, add a **Multi/Sub-Object** node to the active view. In the **Parameter Editor**, click **Set Number**. Set **Number of Materials** to **6** and then click **OK**. Connect all **Standard** materials to the **Muli/Sub-Object** material. Figure E2 shows the node network. Figure E3 shows the maps in the viewport.

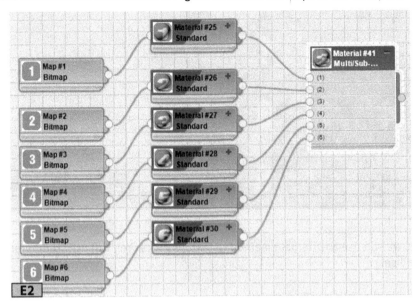

Apply the **Muli/Sub-Object** material to the box in the scene. 3ds Max assigns the maps to the faces of the box. Now, if you want to change a map for a polygon, select that polygon in a viewport and then change the **ID** of the polygon from the **Polygon: Material IDs** rollout of the **Modify** panel.

You can use the **UV Editor** to change the orientation of the map. For example, if you want to change the orientation of the top face [see Figure E4], add **Unwrap UVW** modifier to the stack and then click **Polygon** from the **Selection** rollout. Select the top polygon and click **Open UV Editor** from the **Edit UVs** rollout. Press **A** to enable angel snap and then click **Rotate Selected Subobjects** from the toolbar. Now, rotate the selected polygon by **90** degrees to change the orientation of the map.

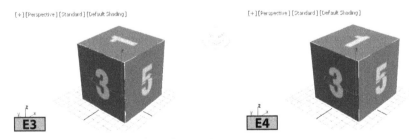

## Exercise 18: Working with the ShapeMap

In this exercise, we will create a resolution independent map using the **ShapeMap**.

The following Table summarizes the exercise.

| Table E18: Working with the ShapeMap | |
|---|---|
| Topics in this section: | • Getting Ready<br>• Working with ShapeMap |
| Skill Level | Beginner |
| Project Folder | **unit-mt2** |
| Final Exercise File | **umt2-hoe18-end.max** |
| Time to Complete | 20 Minutes |

Getting Ready

Open **umt2-hoe18-start.max** in 3ds Max.

Working with the ShapeMap

Press **M** to open the **Slate Material Editor** and then from the **Material/Map Browser | General | Maps** rollout, drag **Standard** to the active view. Connect **ShapeMap** to the **Diffuse** slot of the material. Select the plane in the viewport. RMB click on the material node and then choose **Assign Material to Selection**.

Again, RMB click and then choose **Show Shaded Material in Viewport**. Notice only standard logo is displayed in the viewport at this moment [see Figure E1].

On the **Parameter Editor | ShapeMap | Shape Parameters** rollout, click **None** and then click the apple logo spline in any viewport. The shape is now displayed on the plane in the viewport [see Figure E2]. On the **Closed Shapes** section, turn on the **Render Outline** switch. On the **Outlines** section, set **Width** to **5**.

E1  E2

Set **Fill Color, Line Color, Background Color** to **RGB [141, 141, 141]**, **RGB [252, 255, 0]**, and **RGB [156, 188, 247]**, respectively. On the **Map Boundary** section, select **Manual** and then set **Width** and **Height** to **537**, and **300**, respectively.

The logo is now centered on the plane [see Figure E3]. Take a render [see Figure E4]. Now, if zoom in on an area of the logo and then render, you would notice that you will still get a high resolution output [see Figure E5].

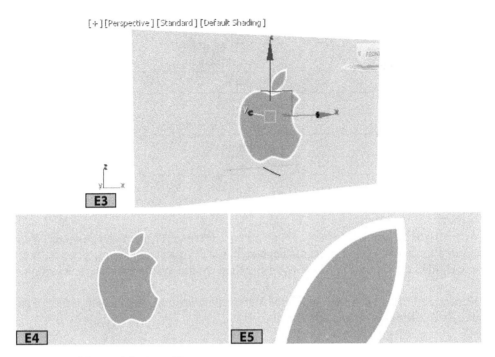

E3

E4

E5

## Exercise 19: Working with Text Map

In this exercise, we will create a resolution independent map using the **Text Map**.

The following Table summarizes the exercise.

| **Table E19:** Working with Text Map | |
|---|---|
| Topics in this section: | • Getting Ready<br>• Working with Text Map |
| Skill Level | Beginner |
| Project Folder | **unit-mt2** |
| Final Exercise File | **umt2-hoe19-end.max** |
| Time to Complete | 20 Minutes |

### Getting Ready

Open **umt2-hoe19-start.max** in 3ds Max.

### Working with the Text Map

Press **M** to open the **Slate Material Editor** and then from the **Material/Map Browser** | **General** | **Maps** rollout, drag **Standard** to the active view. Connect **Text Map** to the **Diffuse** slot of the material. Select the plane in the viewport. RMB click on the material node and then choose **Assign Material to Selection**.

Again, RMB click and then choose **Show Shaded Material in Viewport**. Notice only standard logo is displayed in the viewport at this moment [see Figure E1].

On the **Parameter Editor | Text Map | Text Parameters** rollout, click **None** and then click the **TextPlus** object in any viewport. The text is now displayed on the plane in the viewport [see Figure E2]. On the **Characters** section, turn on the **Render Outline** switch. On the **Outlines** section, set **Width** to **5**.

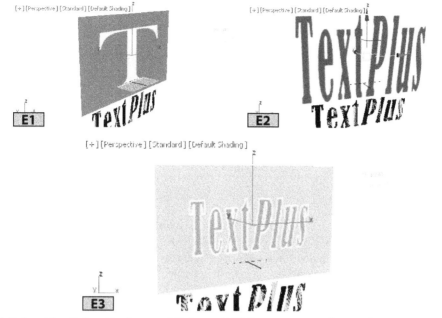

Set **Fill Color**, **Line Color**, **Background Color** to **RGB [141, 141, 141]**, **RGB [252, 255, 0]**, and **RGB [156, 188, 247]**, respectively. On the **Map Boundary** section, select **Manual** and then set **Width** and **Height** to **500**, and **200**, respectively.

The text is now centered on the plane [see Figure E3]. Take a render [see Figure E4]. Now, if zoom in on an area of the text and then render, you would notice that you will still get a high resolution output [see Figure E5].

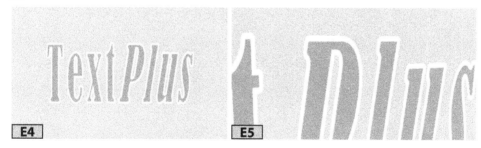

In this exercise, we will create a resolution independent map using the **TextureObjMask** map.

The following Table summarizes the exercise.

| Table E2O: Working with TextureObjMask map | |
|---|---|
| Topics in this section: | • Getting Ready<br>• Working with TextureObjMask Map |
| Skill Level | Beginner |
| Project Folder | **unit-mt2** |
| Final Exercise File | **umt2-hoe2O-end.max** |
| Time to Complete | 20 Minutes |

Getting Ready
Open **umt2-hoe2O-start.max** in 3ds Max.

Working with the TextureObjMask Map
Press **M** to open the **Slate Material Editor** and then drag **TextureObjMask** to the active view. On the **Parameter Editor | TextureObjMask | Parameters** rollout, click **Control Object's None** button and then click on the sphere in a viewport to make it the control object.

Now, drag the **Cellular** and **Noise** maps to the active view. Change the color as desired and then connect Cellular map to the **Texture1** [outside texture] port of the **TextureObjMask** and **Noise** map to the **Texture2** [inside texture] port [see Figure E1]. In the **Parameter Editor | TextureObjMask | Parameters** rollout, set **Transition Range** to **25**.

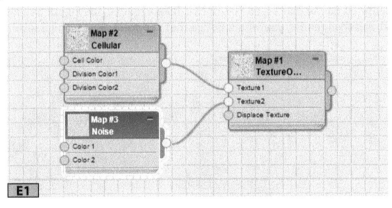

E1

Now, create a **Standard** material and connect its **Diffuse** port to the **TextureObjMask.** Select the plane in a viewport and RMB click on the material node and then choose **Assign Material to Selection**. Again, RMB click and then choose **Show Shaded Material in Viewport**. Take a test render [see Figure E2]. The sphere is obscuring the plane rendering. Create another **Standard** material and set its **Opacity** to **35**. Take a test render [see Figure E3].

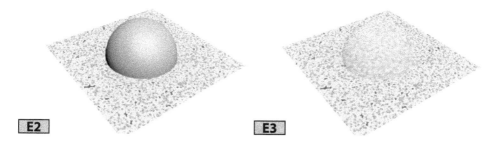

E2

E3

## Summary

The unit covered the following topics:

- General/Scanline materials
- General maps

This page is intentionally left blank

# Index

# Other Books Published by Rising Polygon

Rising Polygon Publishing

[ Best Textbooks at Lower Prices ]

**Modeling Techniques**
with
**3ds Max 2016 and CINEMA 4D R17 Studio**
The Ultimate Beginner's Guide

@risingpolygon
www.risingpolygon.ca

[ Best Textbooks at Lower Prices ]

# Modeling Techniques
## with
# 3ds Max 2017
### The Ultimate Beginner's Guide
#### 2nd Edition

🐦 @risingpolygon
@ www.risingpolygon.co

[ Best Textbooks at Lower Prices ]

**Modeling Techniques**
with
**CINEMA 4D R17 Studio**
The Ultimate Beginner's Guide
2<sup>nd</sup> Edition

@risingpolygon
www.risingpolygon.co

**Modeling Techniques**
with
**3ds Max 2017 and CINEMA 4D R17 Studio**
The Ultimate Beginner's Guide

**2nd Edition**

@risingpolygon
www.risingpolygon.co

[ Best Textbooks at Lower Prices ]

# Texturing Techniques
### with
# 3ds Max 2017
## The Ultimate Beginner's Guide

Contains 3 bonus chapters on creating cutsom maps and textures using Photoshop.

@risingpolygon
www.risingpolygon.co

Rising Polygon Publishing

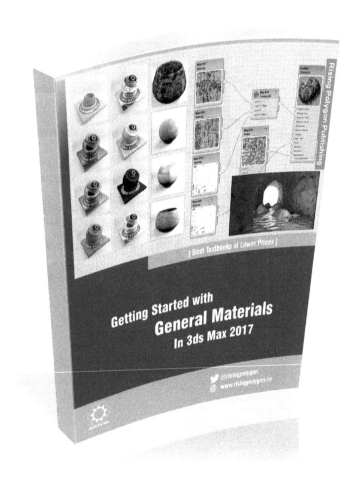

Rising Polygon Publishing

[ Best Textbooks at Lower Prices ]

Getting Started with
Physical, mental ray, and Autodesk Materials
In 3ds Max 2017

@risingpolygon
www.risingpolygon.co

{ Best Textbooks at Lower Prices }

**Modeling and Texturing Techniques**

With

**3ds Max 2017**

The Ultimate Beginner's Guide

* Contains 3 bonus chapters on creating cutsom maps and textures using Photoshop.

@risingpolygon
www.risingpolygon.co

Rising Polygon Publishing

www.ingramcontent.com/pod-product-compliance
Lightning Source LLC
Chambersburg PA
CBHW060454060326
0689CB00020B/4526